EATALY

ALL ABOUT

PIZZA, PANE & PANINI

EATALY

ALL ABOUT
PIZZA, PANE & PANINI

Regional Pizza, Bread & Sandwich Traditions

WRITTEN WITH NATALIE DANFORD
PHOTOGRAPHS BY FRANCESCO SAPIENZA

RIZZOLI
NEW YORK
New York Paris London Milan

CONTENTS

PIZZA ROTONDA 7

Impasto per la Pizza Eataly 10
Pizza Radicchio e Cipolla 21
Impasto per la Pizza Napoletana 24
Pizza Margherita Verace STG 25
Pizza Marinara 33
Calzone 37
Pizza Stella 41
Pizza Fritta 43

Pizza Cacio e Pepe 46
Pizza Tonno e Cipolla 50
Pizza al Tartufo 53
Pizza ai Carciofini 56
Pizza Massese 59
Impasto per la Pizza al Padellino 61
Tiella di Gaeta 66
Pasta Sfoglia per Pizzette 70

PIZZA AL TAGLIO E FOCACCIA 77

Impasto per la Pizza alla Pala 80
Pizza alla Pala di Salsicccia, Peperoni e Cipolla 81
Focaccia Genovese 90
Focaccia di Voltri 93
Focaccia di Recco 101

Focaccia Barese 109
Panzerotti 111
Farinata 113
Schiacciata all'Uva 114
Focaccia Dolce 118

PANINI 123

Pane Rustico 125
Filoncini 128
Rosette 133
Panini Soffici 138
Panino Caprese 145
Pane in Cassetta 147
Tramezzini 150
Panino di Manzo 153

Panino di Porchetta 154
Piadina con Formaggio Fresco e Rucola 158
Crescentine Modenesi 161
Gnocco Fritto 162
Panuozzo 163
Bombolini al Gelato 165
Biscotti al Gelato 168

Index 171

PIZZA ROTONDA

*Fatte 'na pizza c'a pummarola 'ncoppa
vedrai che il mondo poi ti sorriderà.*

*Have yourself a pizza topped with tomatoes,
and the whole world smiles with you.*

— PINO DANIELE

LA PIZZA È UNA COSA SERIA

THE EATALY PIZZA MANIFESTO

THE BASICS ARE IMPORTANT. At Eataly, we use only artisanal, organic flour from Mulino Marino in Cossano Belbo, Cuneo, which for three generations has ground grain while respecting the wheat germ and fibers. For our pizza, we use a mix of semi-whole wheat buratto flour mixed with type 0 flour. For more on various types of flours and how to combine them, see page 18.

WATER COUNTS

We use high hydration because while a wet dough may be a bit more difficult to work with, once baked the crust is softer, honeycombed (full of air bubbles), and more easily digestible. Don't be tempted to over flour your work surface or add too much flour to the dough to make it more manageable. It should be a bit sticky. Get a good bench scraper (a square or rectangular metal blade with a handle) and use it to assist you in moving the dough around when necessary.

LONG FERMENTATION

We start from a *biga*—a pre-ferment or starter dough. That rests for twenty-four hours before it is added to the dough. We use a low quantity of yeast for this *metodo indiretto*, or indirect method, of fermentation.

TIME IS A KEY INGREDIENT

Paradoxically, pizza takes time, but it isn't time-consuming. However, the dough does need time to rise—that is, ferment—so that the flavor and texture develop properly. But making pizza is easy to fit into your day. You control the speed—if you refrigerate the dough, you slow the process. Do you need even more time between mixing up a batch of dough and firing up the oven? Freeze the dough and thaw it when you're ready to use it.

SIMPLE

Our pizzas have few toppings, because we want to bring out the flavor and quality so that each one is recognizable. Pizza dough should never be swimming in sauce or weighed down by an everything-but-the-kitchen-sink series of additions.

WE VALUE THE EARTH

As always, we look for the best local producers, and we make our pizzas only with fresh, seasonal ingredients.

THE WOOD OVEN

Our pizza gets cooked quickly and rigorously in a rotating Marana oven fired with beechwood. The temperature is never too high, to guarantee that the pizza is cooked evenly inside and remains crisp on the outside. If you don't have your own wood-burning oven, we'll show you how to approximate its high temperatures in your standard oven.

GOOD—ACTUALLY, REALLY GOOD!

The ingredients and the process of making it are important, but so is the taste! Our pizza is, above all, good and tasty.

IMPASTO PER LA PIZZA DI EATALY

EATALY PIZZA DOUGH

Makes dough for 4 individual pizzas

We got our start researching all of the different Italian food traditions. For our signature pizza, we took the best of pizza from across Italy to create a meeting point between the grand schools of pizza making in our country. The result is a pizza that is truly "Eatalian." If you have never made a yeasted dough in your life, pizza dough is a great place to start. It is extremely forgiving. It is also extremely flexible. This recipe makes enough dough for four individual pizzas (an Italian pizza is meant to serve one person and is 12 to 14 inches in diameter), but pizza dough freezes nicely and is great to have on hand. However, unless you have an unusually large oven and baking stone, you will be able to bake only one pizza at a time. The recipe was created by head pizzaiolo Francesco Pompilio, who developed the dough, cooking method, and toppings with the support of Eataly executive chef Enrico Panero, flour producer Fulvio Marino, and Slow Food Italia pizza expert Antonio Puzzi.

STARTER

- ⅛ teaspoon instant yeast
- 1½ cups buratto flour

DOUGH

- 1½ cups 0 flour, plus more for work surface
- 2 cups buratto flour
- 1 tablespoon sea salt
- Oil for bowl and pan

TO make the starter, combine the yeast and ⅓ cup water in a large bowl. Stir until dissolved, then gradually add the buratto flour. Stir by hand until smooth and well combined, about 2 minutes. Cover with plastic wrap or a dishtowel and set aside at room temperature for 24 hours.

FOR the dough, combine the flours in a large bowl. Add 1 cup water in a thin stream while mixing. Sprinkle on the salt and mix to combine. Add an additional ⅓ cup water. Add the starter to the dough and knead (or mix in a stand mixer fitted with the dough hook) until smooth and well combined, about 10 minutes.

TRANSFER the dough to an oiled bowl, cover the bowl with plastic wrap or a damp dishtowel, and set aside at room temperature to ferment for 2 hours.

TURN the dough out onto a lightly floured work surface and use a bench scraper to cut it into 4 equal pieces. (If you want to be exact, use a scale to weigh them.)

LIGHTLY oil a tray or baking sheet and set aside. Place 1 piece of dough in front of you on the work surface, smooth side up. Cup the dough with your hands and gently turn it while pressing the edges of the dough underneath so that it forms a round ball with a smooth top stretched tightly. Transfer the rounded dough to the prepared tray or pan and repeat with the remaining dough.

COVER the tray or pan with plastic wrap or a damp dishtowel and let proof at room temperature for 30 minutes, then refrigerate the dough until it is very puffy, at least 8 hours and up to 24 hours.

ABOUT 3 hours before you want to make pizza, remove the dough from the refrigerator and let it sit until it comes back to room temperature.

LE PIZZE DEL TERRITORIO

TELL ME WHAT YOU PUT ON YOUR PIZZA AND I'LL TELL YOU WHO YOU ARE—or at least where you're from. A good pizza dough works like a blank canvas for expressing Italy's strong tradition of eating locally. The origins of pizza famously lie in Napoli (and you can learn the legendary story on page 23), but it's been embraced and adopted up and down the boot, and at Eataly we've come up with a menu of inventive pizzas showcasing regional ingredients made with our signature Eataly dough. Many of the ingredients are DOP, or Denominazione d'Origine Protetta (protected designation of origin), meaning they are produced, processed, and packaged in a specific geographical zone and according to precise tradition, and each step along the way is regulated. Other products are IGP, or Indicazione Geografica Protetta, meaning they hail from a specific area.

PIZZA TRIESTE Focaccia with Dok dall'Ava prosciutto di San Daniele DOP, fresco Montasio DOP, and extra virgin olive oil

PIZZA MILANO Fior di latte mozzarella, pancetta, and soft pannerone Lodigiano DOP cow's milk cheese

PIZZA TORINO Fior di latte mozzarella, Montebore Vallenostra—a mixed cow's and sheep's milk cheese made by stacking three wheels of decreasing size—thinly sliced potatoes, and extra virgin olive oil

PIZZA PIACENZA Fior di latte mozzarella, smoky and sweet honey-cured pancetta, pioppino mushrooms, and local cacio del Po cheese

PIZZA GENOVA Fior di latte mozzarella, toma di pecora Brigasca—a cheese made from the milk of Brigasca sheep, of which only eighteen hundred remain in Liguria—anchovies, and fresh basil

PIZZA FORLÌ Focaccia with prosciutto di Parma DOP, caramelized figs, and formaggio di fossa di Sogliano DOP—a cheese aged in pits dug into rock

PIZZA FIRENZE Focaccia dough topped with lardo di Colonnata IGP, chestnut honey, and shavings of pecorino Toscano DOP

PIZZA ROMA Fior di latte mozzarella, Romanesco broccoli, guanciale, and straccone di Amatrice—a soft yet aged cheese

PIZZA BARI Fior di latte mozzarella, sun-dried tomatoes, cacioricotta cheese, and cardoncelli mushrooms

LA LIEVITAZIONE

THE ONE THING THAT ALMOST EVERY TYPE OF BREAD, including pizza, has in common is that its dough has been fed with some kind of yeast—whether natural or industrially made—and allowed to rise. Most doughs have two rising periods: first with the entire dough still combined, known as the first rise or the fermentation, and then again after the dough has been portioned and shaped into loaves or balls, known as the second rise or proof. Some types of bread rise a third time, and often you will be instructed to allow the dough to rest for brief periods so that the gluten relaxes, making the dough easier to stretch or shape.

But what is actually happening as dough rises? Chemically speaking, when yeast and flour are exposed to liquid, they begin to break down and emit gas, mostly carbon dioxide, which creates bubbles that become trapped in the dough's gluten web. When a dough is properly risen, it not only increases

---

INSTANT YEAST Instant yeast is sold in envelopes containing 2 ¼ teaspoons or 7 grams of beige granules. Despite the name, instant yeast does not work any more quickly than other types of yeast, but it is more powerful, which means you can use less of it. This is preferable because industrially produced yeast can lend a chemical aftertaste when used in large amounts. Instant yeast is also handy because it can be added to the dry ingredients.

ACTIVE DRY YEAST Active dry yeast looks almost identical to instant yeast and is sold in envelopes of the same size, but it is less powerful. It also needs to be hydrated before using, which means it is left to "bloom" in warm (not hot) water for a few minutes. If you want to replace the instant yeast in any recipe in this book with active dry yeast, you will need to use more—about 1½ times as much.

COMPRESSED YEAST Compressed yeast, also known as fresh yeast or cake yeast, is actually the type of yeast used at Eataly and in most professional settings. It comes in a dense 0.6-ounce cube or cake, usually wrapped in foil. Compressed yeast can be inconvenient for home bakers because it begins to lose power very quickly, even when refrigerated. At Eataly, where we use pounds of yeast every day, that's not an issue, but if you're baking bread or pizza once every few weeks, you're going to end up throwing away a lot of yeast. In some parts of the world this is the most commonly available form of yeast, and in other parts (including the United States) it is very difficult for non-professionals to track down. Compressed yeast should be crumbled into warm water and allowed to hydrate before using.

in volume, but also appears lighter and a little bubbly. During fermentation (the first rise), you are usually looking for the dough to double in size. After proofing (the second rise), the dough should feel smooth to the touch and spring back into shape slowly if you poke it gently with a finger. Yeast needs a warm—though not hot—environment to act. Sometimes, though, a longer, slower rise is preferable, as it allows the dough to develop more flavor. In those cases, a recipe will instruct you to refrigerate the dough. (For example, the Impasto per la Pizza di Eataly on page 10 proofs in the refrigerator.) In any case, the duration of the rise is always an estimate, as many different factors come into play. Use your eyes and hands to determine when a dough is ready.

Yeast is sold in many different forms, and you can also make your own natural yeast, or *lievito madre* (see next page). Always store yeast in the refrigerator to maintain freshness, but know that it does lose some of its power as it ages. The recipes in this book use either instant yeast or lievito madre, but you can convert the amount of yeast using the instructions opposite.

LIEVITO MADRE

AT EATALY WE NURTURE AND SELL OUR OWN LIEVITO MADRE, or mother yeast. What is mother yeast? It is a "dough" created from the spontaneous fermentation of flour and water in which Saccharomyces yeast microbes and lactic acid bacteria are formed. (Please don't be put off by the word "bacteria"—these are substances like the bacteria in yogurt. Mother yeast is actually beneficial.) Eataly's natural mother yeast was created by mixing together water and rye flour and leaving the mixture to ferment, allowing microbes to culture from the sugars present in the flour. We "feed" the mother yeast every day with Mulino Marino buratto flour, an organic, stone-ground flour that contains the germ. The germ is the portion of the grain that contains most of the nutrients, which is perfect for maintaining the mother yeast. The mother yeast, like any living being, needs to be fed. Feeding the mother is simple but essential to keeping it alive and active enough to leaven bread. Always take good care of your mother!

Keep your mother yeast in the refrigerator when not in use. At least 4 hours before you plan to use it, remove it from the refrigerator. For every 5 ounces of yeast (½ cup to ¾ cup), add 1 cup buratto flour and ⅔ cup warm water. Stir to combine and allow the mother yeast to sit at room temperature until you are ready to use it. If you go more than one week without using your mother yeast, maintain it by doing the above and then immediately returning it to the refrigerator. If refreshed periodically, the mother yeast will last forever!

IF YOU WANT TO TRY TO MAKE YOUR OWN MOTHER YEAST AT HOME, YOU WILL NEED RYE FLOUR, WATER, AND A LITTLE BIT OF PATIENCE:

1. Stir together equal parts (about ½ cup each) rye flour and water in a glass jar with a tight-fitting lid. At first your starter will look like nothing much. Screw the lid on tightly and set the starter aside for a couple of days at room temperature.

2. The flour will get dark (and a little smelly) and will begin to bubble. Transfer the mixture from the jar to a bowl. Throw out about half of the mixture and wash the jar. Return the reserved mixture to the jar and again stir in equal parts water and rye flour, about ¼ cup this time. Cover and set aside at room temperature.

3. Each time the mixture darkens and bubbles, repeat step 2. It will bubble on an increasingly fast schedule. When it bubbles and almost doubles in size, looks frothy, and smells tart (but not overly alcoholic and "beery") in 8 hours or less after you feed it, you're ready to go. Use your new lievito madre to bake, and store and refresh it as described above.

LA STESURA

YOU'VE MADE YOUR PIZZA DOUGH. It's soft and pillowy with a smooth surface on top and an airy texture. Now comes the fun part: gently stretching the pizza dough by hand into a circle. Pizza dough should never be rolled with a rolling pin.

1. **DUST THE DOUGH WITH FLOUR.** It's okay to dust more heavily at this point, but once you start stretching the dough you want to use a lighter hand.

2. **WORKING GENTLY BUT CONFIDENTLY,** flatten the top of the disk with the palm of one hand. The goal is to transform the dough from a mound into a disk without bursting all of the bubbles you've taken such care to form. Press outward with both hands from the center of the dough while turning until the pizza is 7 to 8 inches in diameter.

3. **TO FINISH STRETCHING,** use the *schiaffo,* or slap, technique: place your left hand facing upward beneath the left side of the dough and use it to pull outward while your right hand slaps the top of the right side of the dough and pushes in the opposite direction while rotating. The perimeter of the dough will remain thicker and form the crust, or *cornicione,* which serves a dual purpose: it works as a barrier to keep any looser toppings from flowing off the surface of the pizza as it cooks, and it provides texture contrast.

4. **REPEAT,** always turning the dough in the same direction, until you have a thin, even circle of dough with a thicker edge.

LA FARINA

FARINA 00

This is Italy's all-purpose flour. In Italy we grade flours by the extraction rate, meaning how much of the bran and germ have been removed, and 00 is the most highly refined. It is also finely ground—if you pinch a little, it feels silky, never sandy or gritty.

FARINA 0

Farina 0 is slightly more coarse than farina 00. It is a lower extraction flour than farina 00, which means it contains some traces of the bran and germ. Farina 0 and farina 00 can substitute for each other (and both can be replaced with unbleached all-purpose flour).

SEMOLA RIMACINATA

Rimacinata means remilled, because this semolina flour is twice-ground to a very fine texture. This is the type of semolina, or durum wheat, flour that you want to use for bread. Coarser semolina is used to make flour-and-water pastas, such as orecchiette, but when this hard wheat is more coarsely ground, the pieces have microscopic sharp edges that cut gluten strands as you're kneading.

FARINA DI CECI

Chickpea flour, used to make farinata, is made from finely ground chickpeas rather than a grain. It has a nutty aroma and flavor and a tawny color.

FARINA BURATTO

Buratto flour from Mulino Marino, a small stone-grinding mill in the village of Cossano Belbo in Piemonte's Langhe area, is sifted by traditional means through a cheesecloth, or buratto. It is made with a special strain of heirloom wheat and contains the complete germ and all of the nutrients, making it, in essence, a whole white flour. It is an excellent choice for bread and pizza.

FARINA INTEGRALE

Whole wheat flour has not had the bran and germ of the wheat sifted out. (It is at the opposite end of the extraction spectrum from farina 00.) This gives it a wheatier taste and a darker color. It also makes it heavier than white flour, which keeps a dough made with whole wheat flour from rising as quickly as a dough made from white flour. Whole wheat flour is "thirstier" than white flour, too, meaning that it absorbs more liquid. Finally, the bran in whole wheat flour has sharp edges, which actually cut the gluten strands that form when you're kneading the dough, affecting the texture. For all of these reasons, a dough—whether for pizza or bread—with 100 percent whole wheat flour will feel dense. You can, however, replace some white flour with whole wheat flour in pizza dough if you like a chewy texture. The dough will require a longer time to rise and puff suitably.

FARINA MANITOBA

Bread flour is made by milling high-protein wheat. It is considered "strong" because of its protein content, which means it contains a large amount of gluten and easily forms an elastic dough. In Italy, high-protein flour is often labeled farina Manitoba or farina d'America, as it is typically made using a strain of wheat that was first grown in Canada.

PIZZA RADICCHIO E CIPOLLA
PIZZA WITH RADICCHIO AND ONION

Makes 4 individual pizzas

You can use our Eataly pizza dough to make any of the pizzas in this book, but we think it really shines with vegetarian choices. Radicchio is a touch bitter when raw, but when cooked briefly it turns sweet and tender. A drizzle of aceto balsamico di Modena—made by aging cooked wine must and vinegar in wooden casks—adds an irresistible umami flavor.

8 ounces buffalo or fior di latte mozzarella

2 small heads radicchio

1 large red onion

½ teaspoon fine sea salt

2 tablespoons olive oil

1 batch Impasto per la Pizza di Eataly (page 10)

Flour for dusting work surface

½ cup grated Parmigiano Reggiano

1 tablespoon balsamic vinegar

CUT the mozzarella into 1-inch cubes. Set a sieve over a bowl and line the sieve with paper towels. Place the mozzarella in the towel-lined sieve and refrigerate for at least 2 hours and up to 8 hours to drain as much excess liquid as possible.

AT least 1 hour before you plan to bake the pizzas, place a rack with a baking stone on the second highest shelf (with no racks above it) and preheat the oven to its highest temperature. Most home ovens go up to at least 500°F; some may go higher. It is important to preheat the oven and the stone at length. If the highest heat you can achieve in your oven is on the broil setting, preheat the oven and stone to 500°F, then switch to the broiler setting before sliding in the pizza. (Alternatively, build a fire in a wood-burning oven and bring to 850°F to 900°F.)

CORE the radicchio and cut into ribbons. Cut the onion in half, then thinly slice into half-moons. Combine the radicchio, onion, salt, and 1 tablespoon olive oil in a bowl and toss to combine.

DUST the top and sides of one of the risen dough rounds generously with flour. With a floured bench scraper, scrape the dough off of the surface and flip it over. Generously dust the dough with additional flour so that both sides are now floured.

STARTING in the center of the dough with your fingers, press down and away from you on the dough to push the air toward the perimeter. Flip the dough again, dusting with more flour as needed to keep it from sticking, and use the same method of pressing from the center to the crust until you have an even circle of dough 7 to 8 inches in diameter. Use the *schiaffo*, or slap, technique by taking your left hand facing upwards beneath the left side of the dough pulling outwards while your right hand slaps the top of the right side of the dough and pushes in the opposite direction while rotating. At this point try to use as little flour as possible without letting your dough stick to the work surface. Once your dough is about 10 inches in diameter you are ready to add the toppings.

SCATTER about one-quarter of the drained mozzarella onto the pizza, leaving a ½-inch margin around the perimeter free of cheese. Top with about one-quarter of the radicchio mixture.

DUST a *pala,* or oven peel, with just enough flour to keep the dough from sticking and slide the pizza onto the peel. Once the pizza is on the peel you can gently stretch it a few more times so that it is 12 inches in diameter. Keep the size of your pizza stone in mind—you don't want the edge of the pizza to flop over the side of the stone. Slide the pizza onto the pizza stone.

COOK, rotating the pizza twice, until the bottom is browned and the dough is blistered, 4 to 7 minutes. (It will cook in 1 to 1½ minutes in a wood-burning oven.) Meanwhile, repeat the process with the remaining dough.

AS you remove each cooked pizza from the oven, scatter on about one-quarter of the Parmigiano. Drizzle with a little of the remaining olive oil and a few drops of balsamic vinegar and serve immediately.

LA VERA PIZZA NAPOLETANA

BORN IN NAPOLI, pizza napoletana is world-famous. This pizza has a rags-to-riches story: it rose from humble street-food origins to become the choice of royalty.

In the 1500s and 1600s, pizza Mastunicola—made with lardo, sheep's cheese shavings, basil, and pork cracklings—was popular in Napoli. Dough topped with whitebait—tiny fish—was also a local treat. But it wasn't until the 1800s that pizza would begin to take the form we know (and love) today. Pizzerias sprang up all over the city, but particularly in the quartieri spagnoli—a once upper-crust and now densely populated, labyrinthine, often raucous neighborhood that to this day remains the perfect place to munch on a low-cost snack while strolling and people watching. Pizza had planted its flag.

Pizza then climbed the food chain when Queen Margherita of Savoy visited Naples in 1889. Italy had only been unified for a few decades at that point, and a visit from the queen was a novelty as well as a great honor. Margherita had heard of the unusual local snack known as pizza, and she requested that one be made for her. The queen loved the pizza (how could she not?) and would remain a fan for life, and the combination quickly caught on throughout the city.

Today, Napoli is serious about protecting the tradition and heritage of its pizzas. The Associazione Verace Pizza Napoletana (True Neapolitan Pizza Association) formed in 1984 to safeguard this important food, to establish certain ground rules, including that pizza napoletana must be round and shaped by hand. In 1997, pizza napoletana received DOC certification, and these days, Neapolitan pizza is protected by Traditional Specialty Guaranteed (TSG) certification. (And in 2017 the art of making pizza napoletana was added to the UNESCO list of intangible cultural heritage.) To be considered a true Neapolitan pizza, the dough must be composed of wheat flour, yeast, salt, and water. It's left to rise for up to twenty-four hours, then shaped by hand into a flat, round disk. After that, it's topped with ingredients (preferably from the Campania region, and including tomatoes and buffalo mozzarella or fior di latte mozzarella) and baked for no more than ninety seconds in a blisteringly hot (around 900°F) wood-burning oven. The result is a soft, elastic heart with a tall, fluffy crust.

So the truth is, unless you have your own wood-burning oven (and if you do, invite us over!) you can't make a pizza napoletana at home that meets all of the criteria. But by using a pizza stone and cranking up your home oven as high as it will go, you can create a very close facsimile.

IMPASTO PER LA PIZZA NAPOLETANA

NEAPOLITAN PIZZA DOUGH

Makes dough for 4 individual pizzas

This is it—the mother of all pizza doughs, made according to the rules. Dough for pizza napoletana takes some forethought, but it's not complicated or difficult. The yeast does most of the work. This recipe makes four 12-inch individual pizzas.

1 tablespoon plus 1 teaspoon fine sea salt

5 cups 00 flour or unbleached all-purpose flour

⅛ teaspoon instant yeast

PLACE 1½ cups plus 1 tablespoon room temperature water in a large mixing bowl. Add the salt and stir by hand until dissolved.

ADD 1 cup of the flour and the yeast and stir until combined. Gradually add the remaining 4 cups flour and turn the dough out onto a wooden work surface. Knead energetically until the gluten structure is well developed, 7 to 12 minutes. (To test the gluten structure, pull off a piece of dough the size of a golf ball and stretch it. If it tears into 2 pieces with a shaggy border between them, the gluten is not yet well enough developed and you should continue to knead it. If instead it forms a translucent sheet—known as a "gluten window"—it's ready.)

SHAPE the dough into a ball with a smooth top and any seams on the bottom. Cover loosely with plastic wrap or a damp dishtowel and allow to rest for 30 to 60 minutes so the gluten is relaxed.

USE a bench scraper to cut the dough into 4 equal pieces. Take one piece of dough and using cupped hands, rotate it against the work surface, gently nudging the bottom toward the center, until a smooth top has formed and is pulled tightly (without tearing) and any seams are underneath. Do not flour the work surface heavily—it's actually preferable for the dough to catch slightly as you are doing this. Repeat with the remaining pieces of dough so that you have 4 taut balls of dough with smooth tops.

COVER the balls of dough with a large overturned bowl and let proof at room temperature until very puffy, 22 to 26 hours.

PIZZA MARGHERITA VERACE STG
TSG PIZZA MARGHERITA

Makes 4 individual pizzas

Invented in Napoli in 1889 to honor Queen Margherita of Savoy, the pizza Margherita has become a symbol of Italy eaten the world over. STG stands for Specialità Tradizionale Garantita, or Traditional Specialty Guaranteed, a type of European certification that protects the integrity of outstanding local products. In other words, this is the real deal. In order to be a true STG pizza, this must use Impasto per la Pizza Napoletana and it must be made in a wood-burning oven, but you can try it in a kitchen oven as well: see the note below for instructions.

14 ounces buffalo mozzarella

1¼ cups canned San Marzano tomatoes and their juice

¾ teaspoon fine sea salt

1 batch Impasto per la Pizza Napoletana (page 24)

Flour for dusting work surface

⅔ cup grated Parmigiano Reggiano

1 tablespoon plus 1 teaspoon extra virgin olive oil

16 fresh basil leaves

CUT the mozzarella into 1-inch cubes. Set a sieve over a bowl and line the sieve with paper towels. Place the mozzarella in the towel-lined sieve and refrigerate for at least 2 hours and up to 8 hours to drain as much excess liquid as possible.

AT least 1 hour before you plan to bake the pizzas, build a fire in a wood-burning oven and bring to 850°F to 900°F.

IN a small bowl combine the tomatoes and salt. Use your hands to crush the tomatoes and mix to combine.

DUST the top and sides of one of the risen dough rounds generously with flour. With a floured bench scraper, scrape the dough off of the surface and flip it over. Generously dust the dough with additional flour so that both sides are now floured.

STARTING in the center of the dough with your fingers, press down and away from you on the dough to push the air toward the perimeter. Flip the dough again, dusting with more flour as needed to keep it from sticking, and use the same method of pressing from the center to the crust until you have an even circle of dough 7 to 8 inches in diameter. Use the *schiaffo*, or slap, technique by taking your left hand facing upwards beneath the left side of the dough pulling outwards while your right hand slaps the top of the right side of the dough and pushes in the opposite direction while rotating. At this point try to use as little flour as possible without letting your dough stick to the work surface. Once your dough is about 10 inches in diameter you are ready to add the toppings.

SPOON about one-quarter of the tomato mixture into the center of the pizza. Move the back of the spoon in a circular motion to spread the sauce evenly around the pizza, but leave the crust bare. Scatter on about one-quarter of the drained mozzarella. Sprinkle on one-quarter of the grated Parmigiano Reggiano and drizzle with olive oil.

DUST a *pala*, or oven peel, with just enough flour to keep the dough from sticking and slide the pizza onto the peel. Once the pizza is on the peel you can gently stretch it a few more times so that it is 12 inches in diameter. Slide the pizza onto the floor of the wood-burning oven.

COOK, rotating the pizza twice, until the bottom is browned and the dough is blistered, 1 to 1½ minutes. Meanwhile, repeat the process with the remaining dough.

SCATTER on the basil and serve immediately.

NOTE: In order to achieve STG status, a pizza must be baked in a wood-burning oven, but you can make a good facsimile of this style of pizza in your home oven. It won't have the smoky flavor or the same char, but it will still be delicious. To do this, place a rack with a baking stone on the second highest shelf (with no racks above it) and preheat the oven to its highest temperature. Most home ovens go up to at least 500°F; some may go higher. If the broiler is the highest setting in your oven, preheat the oven and stone and then switch to the broiler setting just before you slide the pizza into the oven. It is important to preheat the oven and the stone at length. Stretch the dough as described above, but keep the size of your pizza stone in mind—you don't want the edge of the pizza to flop over the side of the stone. Top and bake as described; the pizza should be ready in 4 to 7 minutes, depending how high the oven's temperature can go.

MARGHERITA E CO.

A PIZZA MARGHERITA IS ONE OF THE WORLD'S BEST FOODS, but it also makes a great base. If you do decide to add more to your Margherita, use a light touch and aim for just a scattering of ingredients. Don't weigh down the dough.

PIZZA QUATTRO STAGIONI A four seasons pizza is instantly recognizable, because rather than being combined, the ingredients are separated into four quadrants. (If you were the type of kid who didn't like the foods on your plate touching each other, this one is for you!) We put halved black olives (pick a variety that's not overly salty, as the flavor concentrates further in the oven) in one quadrant, sliced blanched baby artichokes in another, and thinly sliced mushrooms in a third. Then bake, and when the pizza comes out of the oven, add a few slices of prosciutto cotto to the fourth quadrant.

PIZZA CAPRICCIOSA *Capricciosa* means capricious, or at the whim of the chef, so this pizza technically could include almost anything, but at Eataly and in most pizzerias it is made with the same ingredients used in a quattro stagioni, but scattered randomly (capriciously) rather than segregated into their own areas: Scatter thinly sliced mushrooms and (pitted) black olives and wedges of blanched baby artichokes over the pizza before baking. When it comes out of the oven, top with a few artfully draped slices of prosciutto cotto.

PIZZA CON FUNGHI Scatter thinly sliced mushrooms (a mandoline is handy for this) over the mozzarella before baking. They will cook in the heat of the oven. Button mushrooms work well, but if you are lucky enough to have a few slices of porcini mushrooms on hand, they are a wonderful choice.

ROSSA O BIANCA?

THOUGH WE ALWAYS LOVE THE CLASSICS, you can put almost anything on top of a pizza. Most pizzeria menus in Italy (and those at Eataly all over the world) are divided into two sections: pizze rosse, or red pizzas, and pizze bianche, or white pizzas. Those color categories aren't literal. In Italian, a red pizza is one with tomato sauce, and a white pizza is one without tomato sauce.

PIZZA ROSSA

"Tomato sauce" is actually a bit of a misnomer. The slick of crushed tomatoes that is spread on an Italian pizza isn't precooked. It usually consists simply of canned tomatoes (preferably the juicy and flavorful San Marzano variety from the Campania region, the birthplace of pizza) mixed with salt. And an Italian pizza is never swimming in sauce—the tomato lightly coats the dough. That allows the complex flavor of the crust to shine through. It's hard to believe that tomatoes—so closely identified with Italian cuisine—are not native to Europe, let alone Italy. We can thank explorers who visited the Americas for bringing back the almost-magical plant in the early sixteenth century. Italians named the round fruit—an especially acidic yellow variety—pomo d'oro, which translates to "golden apple." Wary of poisonous produce, northern Italians didn't fall for the tomato immediately; however, the less affluent southern regions eventually warmed up to the versatile ingredient. The Mediterranean climate offered an ideal growing environment, and farmers began to experiment with more varieties. Today, pomodori are grown across Italy.

PIZZA BIANCA

Another local product from Campania, this one crucial to pizza bianca, is cheese, and specifically mozzarella. Mozzarella di bufala, a DOP product, is made from the milk of Italian water buffaloes; fior di latte mozzarella is made from cow's milk. Both are tender, with an almost custard-like texture. They are delicious eaten plain, but you don't want a pool of water in the middle of your pizza to make the crust soggy, so we recommend dicing and draining them before using them to top a pizza.

PIZZA A PORTAFOGLIO

WITH ALL THIS TALK OF INDIVIDUAL PIZZAS, you may be wondering about the slice. The pizzaioli of Napoli have something even better to offer: pizza a portafoglio, or wallet pizza, folded into quarters, gripped in butcher's paper with the open side pointing upward, and enjoyed while strolling down the street. Antica Pizzeria Port'Alba in Napoli claims to have invented this ingenious snack.

To make a pizza a portafoglio, follow the recipe for pizza Margherita but use only 1 cup canned tomatoes for four pizzas. When the pizza is cooked, remove it from the oven and scatter on basil. Fold the pizza in half to form a semi-circle and in half the other way to form a triangle. Wrap in butcher's paper with the open end out. Try not to burn your tongue as you bite into four layers of pizza goodness!

FIOR DI LATTE MOZZARELLA

At Eataly we make fresh fior di latte mozzarella every day. We learned from the best: we visited Caseificio Olanda in Andria, Puglia to learn the art of making mozzarella, and we follow their process using 100 percent local milk. Our resident mozzarella makers start at ten o'clock in the morning to begin production for our restaurants and customers. First they make the curd, then separate the curd and the liquid by pushing them through a *chitarra,* an instrument shaped like a guitar. The curd is then combined with hot salted water. The mixture is stirred and stretched by hand to ensure an even consistency. The result is fresh, creamy, and perfect for topping our pizzas—or enjoying as is.

Other cheeses work well with pizza, too: hard cheeses such as Parmigiano Reggiano and Grana Padano, both of them DOP products, can be shaved with a vegetable peeler and scattered on top of a cooked pizza for extra savory goodness.

PIZZA MARINARA

PIZZA MARINARA

Makes 4 individual pizzas

The king of the pizze rosse. Marinara means sailor-style, and simple tomato sauce earned this name because sailors could easily transport the necessary ingredients on board. Along with pizza Margherita, this is a Neapolitan classic. You can also include a few anchovy fillets, oregano, and capers for what is often called a pizza napoletana, though in Napoli it is usually labeled a pizza romana. Go figure.

1¼ cups canned San Marzano tomatoes and their juice

¾ teaspoon fine sea salt

4 cloves garlic

1 batch Impasto per la Pizza Napoletana (page 24)

Flour for dusting work surface

1 tablespoon plus 1 teaspoon dried oregano

1 tablespoon plus 1 teaspoon extra virgin olive oil

AT least 1 hour before you plan to bake the pizzas, place a rack with a baking stone on the second highest shelf (with no racks above it) and preheat the oven to its highest temperature. Most home ovens go up to at least 500°F; some may go higher. It is important to preheat the oven and the stone at length. If the highest heat you can achieve in your oven is on the broil setting, preheat the oven and stone to 500°F, then switch to the broiler setting before sliding in the pizza. (Alternatively, build a fire in a wood-burning oven and bring to 850°F to 900°F.)

IN a small bowl combine the tomatoes and salt. Use your hands to crush the tomatoes and mix to combine. Thinly slice the garlic and set aside.

DUST the top and sides of one of the risen dough rounds generously with flour. With a floured bench scraper, scrape the dough off of the surface and flip it over. Generously dust the dough with additional flour so that both sides are now floured.

STARTING in the center of the dough with your fingers, press down and away from you on the dough to push the air toward the perimeter. Flip the dough again, dusting with more flour as needed to keep it from sticking, and use the same method of pressing from the center to the crust until you have an even circle of dough 7 to 8 inches in diameter. Use the *schiaffo*, or slap, technique by taking your left hand facing upwards beneath the left side of the dough pulling outwards while your right hand slaps the top of the right side of the dough and pushes in the opposite direction while rotating. At this point try to use as little flour as possible without letting your dough stick to the work surface. Once your dough is about 10 inches in diameter you are ready to add the toppings.

SPOON about one-quarter of the tomato mixture into the center of the pizza. Move the back of the spoon in a circular motion to spread the sauce evenly around the pizza, but leave the crust bare. Scatter on one-quarter of the garlic. Sprinkle on 1 teaspoon of the oregano and drizzle with olive oil.

DUST a *pala*, or oven peel, with just enough flour to keep the dough from sticking and slide the pizza onto the peel. Once the pizza is on the peel you can gently stretch it a few more times so that it is 12 inches in diameter. Keep the size of your pizza stone in mind—you don't want the edge of the pizza to flop over the side of the stone. Slide the pizza onto the pizza stone.

COOK, rotating the pizza twice, until the bottom is browned and the dough is blistered, 4 to 7 minutes. (It will cook in 1 to 1½ minutes in a wood-burning oven.) Meanwhile, repeat the process with the remaining dough.

SERVE immediately.

CALZONE

CALZONE

Makes 4 individual turnovers

A calzone (the word derives from Neapolitan dialect for trouser leg) is a baked turnover made by folding a round of pizza dough in half. It can be filled with almost anything that you would put on top of an open-face pizza, though this combination is a classic. Because the dough is doubled over it takes slightly longer to cook: 2 to 3 minutes in a wood-burning oven and up to 10 in a standard oven. Be sure to seal the edges well to prevent leakage.

8½ ounces buffalo mozzarella

½ cup canned San Marzano tomatoes, drained

½ teaspoon fine sea salt, plus more to taste

1 batch Impasto per la Pizza Napoletana (page 24)

Flour for dusting work surface

1 cup ricotta

Freshly ground black pepper to taste

⅔ cup grated Parmigiano Reggiano

7 ounces thinly sliced Felino salami

1 tablespoon plus 1 teaspoon extra virgin olive oil

CUT the mozzarella into 1-inch cubes. Set a sieve over a bowl and line the sieve with paper towels. Place the mozzarella in the towel-lined sieve and refrigerate for at least 2 hours and up to 8 hours to drain as much excess liquid as possible.

AT least 1 hour before you plan to bake the calzoni, place a rack with a baking stone on the second highest shelf (with no racks above it) and preheat the oven to its highest temperature. Most home ovens go up to at least 500°F; some may go higher. It is important to preheat the oven and the stone at length. If the highest heat you can achieve in your oven is on the broil setting, preheat the oven and stone to 500°F, then switch to the broiler setting before sliding in the pizza. (Alternatively, build a fire in a wood-burning oven and bring to 850°F to 900°F.)

IN a small bowl combine the tomatoes and ½ teaspoon salt. Use your hands to crush the tomatoes and mix to combine.

DUST the top and sides of one of the risen dough rounds generously with flour. With a floured bench scraper, scrape the dough off of the surface and flip it over. Generously dust the dough with additional flour so that both sides are now floured.

STARTING in the center of the dough with your fingers, press down and away from you on the dough to push the air toward the perimeter. Flip the dough again, dusting with more flour as needed to keep it from sticking, and use the same method of pressing from the center to the crust until you have an even circle of dough 7 to 8 inches in diameter. Use the *schiaffo*, or slap, technique by taking your left hand facing upwards beneath the left side of the dough pulling outwards while your right hand slaps the top of the right side of the dough and pushes in the opposite direction while rotating. At this point try to use as little flour as possible without letting your dough stick to the work surface. Once the dough is a circle about 10 inches in diameter you are ready to add the toppings.

SPOON about ¼ cup of the ricotta into the center of the dough and spread it upwards and around the top half of the circle of dough with the back of the spoon. Be careful not to get any toppings on the perimeter, otherwise the dough will not seal properly. Season the ricotta with a pinch of salt and freshly ground black pepper. Sprinkle on one-quarter of the mozzarella and 1 tablespoon grated Parmigiano. Arrange one-quarter of the salami in a single layer. Once the ingredients are on the top half of the circle of dough, lift the bottom half of the dough and neatly fold it over the top half. Starting at one corner, begin to work your way around, pinching the crust together to seal the turnover. When you are 2 inches from the opposite corner, gently press to expel any air trapped inside, then finish sealing. Go back around once more, pressing firmly to make sure the crust is sealed completely. Spread 2 tablespoons of the tomato mixture on top of the sealed turnover. Sprinkle on a little more Parmigiano and drizzle with olive oil.

DUST a *pala*, or oven peel, with just enough flour to keep the dough from sticking (high-volume professional pizzerias sometimes use metal models) and slide the calzone onto the peel. Once the calzone is on the peel you can gently nudge it into place so that it is an even half-moon shape. Slide it onto the pizza stone.

COOK, rotating the calzone once, until the crust is browned, 7 to 10 minutes. (It will cook in 2 to 3 minutes in a wood-burning oven.) Meanwhile, repeat the process with the remaining dough.

SERVE immediately.

PIZZA STELLA
STAR-SHAPED PIZZA

Makes 4 individual pizzas

We talk a lot about tradition at Eataly, but we're not averse to trying something new and innovative, like this clever pizza that starts out round but ends up star-shaped. Certain ingredients are always placed on a pizza after it comes out of the oven, as even a short time in the intense heat of a pizza oven would be too much for them. One of those is arugula, which is wilted ever so slightly by the heat of the pizza but maintains its fresh taste; another is prosciutto crudo, which should never, ever be cooked. If you have some on hand, it makes a nice addition to this pizza.

1 cup canned San Marzano tomatoes and their juice

1 teaspoon fine sea salt, divided

3 ounces Grana Padano

11 ounces cherry tomatoes

6 ounces baby arugula, preferably wild

3 tablespoons extra virgin olive oil

1 batch Impasto per la Pizza Napoletana (page 24)

Flour for dusting work surface

AT least 1 hour before you plan to bake the pizzas, place a rack with a baking stone on the second highest shelf (with no racks above it) and preheat the oven to its highest temperature. Most home ovens go up to at least 500°F; some may go higher. It is important to preheat the oven and the stone at length. If the highest heat you can achieve in your oven is on the broil setting, preheat the oven and stone to 500°F, then switch to the broiler setting before sliding in the pizza. (Alternatively, build a fire in a wood-burning oven and bring to 850°F to 900°F.)

IN a small bowl combine the San Marzano tomatoes and ½ teaspoon salt. Use your hands to crush the tomatoes and mix to combine. Shave about half of the Grana Padano with a vegetable peeler. Halve the cherry tomatoes. In a large bowl toss the arugula and the cherry tomatoes with the cheese shavings. Toss with 1 tablespoon of the olive oil and the remaining ½ teaspoon salt and set aside.

DUST the top and sides of one of the risen dough rounds generously with flour. With a floured bench scraper, scrape the dough off of the surface and flip it over. Generously dust the dough with additional flour so that both sides are now floured.

STARTING in the center of the dough with your fingers, press down and away from you on the dough to push the air toward the perimeter. Flip the dough again, dusting with more flour as needed to keep it from sticking, and use the same method of pressing from the center to the crust until you have an even circle of dough 7 to 8 inches in diameter. Use the *schiaffo*, or slap, technique by taking your left hand facing upwards beneath the left side of the dough pulling outwards while your right hand slaps the top of the right side of the dough and pushes in the opposite direction while rotating. At this point try to use as little flour as possible without letting your dough stick to the work surface. Once your dough is about 10 inches in diameter you are ready to add the toppings.

SPOON about one-quarter of the San Marzano tomato mixture into the center of the pizza. Move the back of the spoon in a circular motion to spread the sauce evenly around the pizza, but leave the crust bare. Drizzle with olive oil.

DUST a *pala*, or wooden baking peel, with just enough flour to keep the dough from sticking and slide the pizza onto the peel. Once the pizza is on the peel you can gently stretch it a few more times so that it is 12 inches in diameter. Slide the pizza onto the pizza stone.

COOK, rotating the pizza twice, until the bottom is browned and the dough is blistered, 4 to 7 minutes. (It will cook in 1½ to 2 minutes in a wood-burning oven.) Meanwhile, repeat the process with the remaining dough.

WHEN you remove the first pizza, immediately slice it into 6 wedges. Rotate the wedges so the points are around the outside of the plate (in other words, it is shaped like a star). Pile one-quarter of the arugula and cherry tomato mixture in the center of the star and grate the remaining cheese on top.

SERVE immediately.

PIZZA FRITTA
FRIED PIZZA

Makes 4 individual pizzas

In addition to being pizza mavens and originators, napoletani are big on frying. The streets of the quartieri spagnoli are lined not just with old-school pizzerias but also with *friggitorie,* or fry-shops. You can buy a paper cone with fried croquettes, fried fish and seafood, or fried vegetables. Or you can combine these two excellent traditions and indulge in a fried pizza. The recipe below is for the turnover type of fried pizza; a montanara is a fried disk of dough that is then slicked with tomato sauce, topped with mozzarella, and baked briefly to melt the cheese. In Napoli, peanut oil is the top choice for frying pizza, but you can also obtain good results with sunflower or canola oil. Just don't be stingy, and use an instant-read thermometer to measure the oil's temperature.

8½ ounces buffalo mozzarella

¾ cup canned San Marzano tomatoes in their juice

½ teaspoon fine sea salt, plus more to taste

Oil for frying

1 batch Impasto per la Pizza Napoletana (page 24)

Flour for dusting work surface

1 cup ricotta

Freshly ground black pepper

⅔ cup grated Parmigiano Reggiano

Fresh basil leaves

CUT the mozzarella into 1-inch cubes. Set a sieve over a bowl and line the sieve with paper towels. Place the mozzarella in the towel-lined sieve and refrigerate for at least 2 hours and up to 8 hours to drain as much excess liquid as possible.

WHEN you are ready to make the pizzas, in a small bowl combine the tomatoes and ½ teaspoon salt. Use your hands to crush the tomatoes and mix to combine. Line a pan with paper towels and set aside.

FILL a high-sided heavy pot with several inches of oil for frying. Over medium heat, bring to 375°F.

DUST the top and sides of one of the risen dough rounds generously with flour. With a floured bench scraper, scrape the dough off of the surface and flip it over. Generously dust the dough with additional flour so that both sides are now floured.

STARTING in the center of the dough with your fingers, press down and away from you on the dough to push the air toward the perimeter. Flip the dough again, dusting with more flour as needed to keep it from sticking, and use the same method of pressing from the center to the crust until you have an even circle of dough 7 to 8 inches in diameter. Use the *schiaffo*, or slap, technique by taking your left hand facing upwards beneath the left side of the dough pulling outwards while your right hand slaps the top of the right side of the dough and pushes in the opposite direction while rotating. At this point try to use as little flour as possible without letting your dough stick to the work surface. Once your dough is about 10 inches in diameter you are ready to add the toppings.

SPOON about ¼ cup of the ricotta into the center of the dough and spread it upwards and around the top half of the circle of dough with the back of the spoon. Be careful not to get any toppings on the perimeter, otherwise the dough will not seal properly. Season the ricotta with a pinch of salt and freshly ground black pepper. Sprinkle on one-quarter of the mozzarella, one-quarter of the grated Parmigiano Reggiano, and a few basil leaves. Finally, top the ingredients with two spoonfuls of the tomato mixture. Once all of the ingredients are on the top half of your pizza, lift the bottom half of the dough and neatly fold it over the top half to make a half-moon turnover. Starting at one corner, begin to work your way around, pinching the crust together to seal the turnover. When you are 2 inches from the opposite corner, gently press to expel any air trapped inside, then finish sealing. Go back around once more, pressing firmly to make sure the crust is sealed completely.

CAREFULLY slide the turnover into the hot oil. Using a slotted spoon or skimmer turn the turnover often while frying to make sure it is cooking evenly on all sides, and keep an eye on the oil temperature, adjusting the heat as necessary to keep it at 375°F. Fry until golden, about 3 minutes. Remove with the slotted spoon or skimmer and drain briefly on the prepared pan. Repeat with remaining dough and filling. If you have a large enough pot you can fry more than one pizza at a time, but be sure the temperature of the oil doesn't dip too low, and don't crowd the pot.

SERVE immediately.

PIZZA ROMANA TONDA

NAPOLI MAY BE THE BIRTHPLACE OF PIZZA, but pizza napoletana is far from the only game in town. Roma, too, is famous for its pizza. The Roman pizza sometimes known as pinza is made of a dough that is light, airy, fluffy, and crunchy all at once, typically formed into a rectangle. That's the type of dough we use for our pizza alla pala (see page 80).

But the Eternal City also offers pizza romana tonda, or round Roman pizza, which has a cracker-like crust that is crisp rather than pillowy and famed for its *scrochiarella*—the crunching sound it makes as you eat it. If you cut a wedge of Neapolitan pizza and hold it up in the air, the pointed tip will sag, but a wedge of pizza romana tonda should never sag.

This type of crisp crust is made with a dough that incorporates less water than other pizza doughs, and it doesn't rise for long; it also is made with oil in the dough, not just brushed or drizzled on top, all with aim of achieving that crunch. Unlike the puffy *cornicione* on a Neapolitan pizza, the rim of a pizza romana tonda is flat and matte in color. The dough is stretched a bit thinner as well.

PIZZA CACIO E PEPE

CACIO E PEPE PIZZA

Makes 4 individual pizzas

Spaghetti robed in a silky sauce of cacio e pepe—cheese and black pepper—is one of Roma's most famous pasta dishes. The same combination works well as a topping for a satisfying pizza bianca. (This is also a good choice for pizza alla pala, page 80, especially if you are making a selection of pizzas for a crowd.)

5 ounces fior di latte or buffalo mozzarella

1 batch Impasto per la Pizza di Eataly (page 10)

Flour for dusting work surface

¾ cup grated pecorino romano

Freshly ground black pepper

Fresh basil leaves

2 tablespoons extra virgin olive oil

CUT the mozzarella into 1-inch cubes. Set a sieve over a bowl and line the sieve with paper towels. Place the mozzarella in the towel-lined sieve and refrigerate for at least 2 hours and up to 8 hours to drain as much excess liquid as possible.

AT least 1 hour before you plan to bake the pizzas, place a rack with a baking stone on the second highest shelf (with no racks above it) and preheat the oven to its highest temperature. Most home ovens go up to at least 500°F; some may go higher. It is important to preheat the oven and the stone at length. If the highest heat you can achieve in your oven is on the broil setting, preheat the oven and stone to 500°F, then switch to the broiler setting before sliding in the pizza. (Alternatively, build a fire in a wood-burning oven and bring to 850°F to 900°F.)

DUST the top and sides of one of the risen dough rounds generously with flour. With a floured bench scraper, scrape the dough off of the surface and flip it over. Generously dust the dough with additional flour so that both sides are now floured.

STARTING in the center of the dough with your fingers, press down and away from you to flatten the dough. Flip the dough again, dusting with more flour as needed to keep it from sticking, and use the same method of pressing from the center outward until you have an even circle of dough 7 to 8 inches in diameter. Use the *schiaffo*, or slap, technique by taking your left hand facing upwards beneath the left side of the dough pulling outwards while your right hand slaps the top of the right side of

the dough and pushes in the opposite direction while rotating. At this point try to use as little flour as possible without letting your dough stick to the work surface. Once your dough is about 10 inches in diameter and very thin, you are ready to add the toppings.

SCATTER about one-quarter of the mozzarella over the surface of the dough, leaving a ½-inch border around the perimeter free of cheese.

DUST a *pala*, or oven peel, with just enough flour to keep the dough from sticking and slide the pizza onto the peel. Once the pizza is on the peel you can gently stretch it a few more times so that it is 12 inches in diameter. Slide the pizza onto the pizza stone.

COOK, rotating the pizza twice, until the bottom is browned and the dough is crisp, 4 to 6 minutes. (It will cook in 1½ to 2 minutes in a wood-burning oven.) Meanwhile, repeat the process with the remaining dough.

AS soon as you remove the pizza from the oven, scatter on about one-quarter of the grated cheese and season very generously with black pepper. Scatter on a few basil leaves and drizzle with one-quarter of the olive oil.

SERVE immediately.

UN PRIMO DIVENTA PIZZA

CACIO E PEPE isn't the only pasta sauce that can conveniently transform into a pizza topping. Try any of the following classics:

PIZZA ALL'AMATRICIANA: Amatrice is a small town in Lazio—the region where Roma is located—famed for this savory, slightly spicy mix. Spread hand-crushed canned tomatoes over the surface of the dough. Thinly slice red onions and toss with chili flakes and olive oil, then spread over the tomato mixture. Sauté cubes or matchsticks of guanciale (cured pork jowl) until crisp. As you remove each pizza from the oven, sprinkle on the guanciale, grated Parmigiano Reggiano, and minced parsley. Drizzle with a little olive oil.

PIZZA ALLA GRICIA: Gricia is similar to Amatriciana, but without the tomato mixture. Top the unbaked dough with sliced red onions sautéed with guanciale. Finish with grated pecorino romano, coarsely ground black pepper, and olive oil. Sprinkle on additional cheese after baking.

PIZZA CARBONARA: In a skillet, sauté cubes of guanciale until they begin to render their fat. Add beaten eggs seasoned lightly with salt and pepper and a handful of grated Parmigiano and cook until just set. Scatter drained cubes of mozzarella on the dough. Top with the egg and guanciale mixture and bake the pizza. Remove from the oven and add more Parmigiano, a generous amount of freshly ground black pepper (the "coal dust" that gives the dish its name), and minced parsley.

PIZZA AI CINQUE FORMAGGI: Four cheeses is the standard, but we like to go over the top and use five different kinds of cheese on this decadent pizza. Scatter cubed mozzarella on the dough. Top with grated Parmigiano, grated aged pecorino, crumbled pungent gorgonzola, and shredded provolone and bake. Garnish with freshly snipped chives after baking.

PIZZA TONNO E CIPOLLA
TUNA AND ONION PIZZA

Makes 4 individual pizzas

As the most delicious tuna melt you've ever eaten, this pizza breaks one of the cardinal rules of Italian cooking by combining fish with cheese. You can scatter a few rinsed and drained capers on top with the onions if you like. If you can get your hands on sweet torpedo-shaped red Tropea onions, use them here.

8 ounces fior di latte or buffalo mozzarella

1 cup canned San Marzano tomatoes and their juice

½ teaspoon fine sea salt

1 yellow onion

1 6-ounce jar tuna in olive oil

1 batch Impasto per la Pizza di Eataly (page 10)

Flour for dusting work surface

1 tablespoon salted capers, rinsed and drained

1 tablespoon extra virgin olive oil

CUT the mozzarella into 1-inch cubes. Set a sieve over a bowl and line the sieve with paper towels. Place the mozzarella in the towel-lined sieve and refrigerate for at least 2 hours and up to 8 hours to drain as much excess liquid as possible.

AT least 1 hour before you plan to bake the pizzas, place a rack with a baking stone on the second highest shelf (with no racks above it) and preheat the oven to its highest temperature. Most home ovens go up to at least 500°F; some may go higher. It is important to preheat the oven and the stone at length. If the highest heat you can achieve in your oven is on the broil setting, preheat the oven and stone to 500°F, then switch to the broiler setting before sliding in the pizza. (Alternatively, build a fire in a wood-burning oven and bring to 850°F to 900°F.)

IN a small bowl combine the tomatoes and salt. Use your hands to crush the tomatoes and mix to combine. Cut the onion in half lengthwise and then slice into half-moons. Separate the pieces and set aside. Drain the tuna of excess oil and gently flake with a fork.

DUST the top and sides of one of the risen dough rounds generously with flour. With a floured bench scraper, scrape the dough off of the surface and flip it over. Generously dust the dough with additional flour so that both sides are now floured.

STARTING in the center of the dough with your fingers, press down and away from you to flatten the dough. Flip the dough again, dusting with more flour as needed to keep it from sticking, and use the same method of pressing from the center outward until you have an even circle of dough 7 to 8 inches in diameter. Use the *schiaffo*, or slap, technique by taking your left hand facing upwards beneath the left side of the dough pulling outwards while your right hand slaps the top of the right side of the dough and pushes in the opposite direction while rotating. At this point try to use as little flour as possible without letting your dough stick to the work surface. Once your dough is about 10 inches in diameter and very thin, you are ready to add the toppings.

SPOON about one-quarter of the tomato mixture into the center of the pizza. Move the back of the spoon in a circular motion to spread the sauce evenly around the pizza, but leave the crust bare. Scatter on about one-quarter of the drained mozzarella. Scatter on one-quarter of the tuna and one-quarter of the onion. Sprinkle on the capers and drizzle with oil.

DUST a *pala*, or oven peel, with just enough flour to keep the dough from sticking and slide the pizza onto the peel. Once the pizza is on the peel you can gently stretch it a few more times so that it is 12 inches in diameter. Slide the pizza onto the pizza stone.

COOK, rotating the pizza twice, until the bottom is browned and the dough is blistered, 4 to 6 minutes. (It will cook in 1½ to 2 minutes in a wood-burning oven.) Meanwhile, repeat the process with the remaining dough.

SERVE immediately.

PIZZA AL TARTUFO

TRUFFLE PIZZA

Makes 4 individual pizzas

Thinly shaved petals of truffle give an intoxicating aroma as they land on this simple white pizza. (The acidity of tomatoes would clash with the strong flavor of the truffle.) We're crazy about truffles, one of Italy's great natural delicacies. These bumpy little knobs—known as the "diamonds of the kitchen"—may not look like much when they're dug up painstakingly from the earth, but they add phenomenal flavor to all kinds of dishes. White truffles from Alba are rich and aromatic, while black truffles are delicate and earthy. You can use whichever is in season on this unusual pizza. This makes an elegant appetizer when cut into wedges.

4 ounces fior di latte or buffalo mozzarella

1 batch Impasto per la Pizza di Eataly (page 10) or Impasto per la Pizza Napoletana (page 24)

Flour for dusting work surface

½ cup grated Parmigiano Reggiano

1 tablespoon extra virgin olive oil

1 small black or white truffle (see below)

CUT the mozzarella into 1-inch cubes. Set a sieve over a bowl and line the sieve with paper towels. Place the mozzarella in the towel-lined sieve and refrigerate for at least 2 hours and up to 8 hours to drain as much excess liquid as possible.

AT least 1 hour before you plan to bake the pizzas, place a rack with a baking stone on the second highest shelf (with no racks above it) and preheat the oven to its highest temperature. Most home ovens go up to at least 500°F; some may go higher. It is important to preheat the oven and the stone at length. If the highest heat you can achieve in your oven is on the broil setting, preheat the oven and stone to 500°F, then switch to the broiler setting before sliding in the pizza. (Alternatively, build a fire in a wood-burning oven and bring to 850°F to 900°F.)

DUST the top and sides of one of the risen dough rounds generously with flour. With a floured bench scraper, scrape the dough off of the surface and flip it over. Generously dust the dough with additional flour so that both sides are now floured.

STARTING in the center of the dough with your fingers, press down and away from you to flatten the dough. Flip the dough again, dusting with more flour as needed to keep it from sticking, and use the same method of pressing from the center outward until you have an even circle of dough 7 to 8 inches in diameter. Use the *schiaffo*, or slap, technique by taking your left hand facing upwards beneath the left side of the dough pulling outwards while your right hand slaps the top of the right side of the dough and pushes in the opposite direction while rotating. At this point try to use as little flour as possible without letting your dough stick to the work surface. Once your dough is about 10 inches in diameter and very thin, you are ready to add the toppings.

SCATTER on about one-quarter of the drained mozzarella and 2 tablespoons of the Parmigiano. Drizzle with oil.

DUST a *pala*, or oven peel, with just enough flour to keep the dough from sticking and slide the pizza onto the peel. Once the pizza is on the peel you can gently stretch it a few more times so that it is 12 inches in diameter. Slide the pizza onto the pizza stone.

COOK, rotating the pizza twice, until the bottom is browned and the dough is blistered, 4 to 6 minutes. (It will cook in 1½ to 2 minutes in a wood-burning oven.) Meanwhile, repeat the process with the remaining dough.

AS soon as the pizza is baked, remove it from the oven and thinly shave truffle over the top using a truffle shaver or mandoline on the thinnest setting.

SERVE immediately.

TARTUFO

TRUFFLES ARE TUBERS THAT GROW A FEW INCHES UNDERGROUND. They thrive close to the roots of hardwood trees like oaks, hazelnut, and chestnut. Part of what makes truffles so complex—and enticing—is that their aromas are actually a bouquet of many scents, based on where the truffle grows. This is why truffles from Umbria might smell and taste more garlicky, while truffles from Piemonte might have a more delicate, even floral scent.

White truffles are the most desired for their unforgettable flavor. They have a firm flesh and pale golden color. White truffle season is from September to December when they grow wild in the forests around Alba. Eataly also carries black truffles.

Truffles are best enjoyed as fresh as possible, so you can fully experience the full deep aromas and earthy flavors. Don't wait more than two to three days to enjoy after you receive your whole truffle, and never buy a pre-cut one, unless you plan to use it immediately.

When it comes to storage, avoid moisture at all costs. Place the prized ingredient in clean tissue paper or a breathable container at room temperature in a dark space. Change the tissue paper daily to avoid the build-up of moisture and to retain aroma. Do not freeze your truffle: it will accumulate moisture and lose its aroma. We also recommend that you store your truffle on its own. Products like rice or salt will absorb its aroma, so especially avoid them (unless you intend to flavor the rice or salt with truffle).

Finally, you're ready to eat. As your truffle has oxidized, it may have become slightly reddish. This is natural and healthy. When it comes to how to clean truffles, there is at least one certain rule: do not use water or soap. Instead, remove any dirt with a soft brush. Pro tip: we learned firsthand that official truffle hunters often use a toothbrush. Thinly shave the truffle just before serving using a dedicated shaver or mandoline.

PIZZA AI CARCIOFINI

ARTICHOKE PIZZA

Makes 4 individual pizzas

Carciofini, or baby artichokes, are incorporated into many traditional pizzas, such as quattro stagioni (see page 29). Here they are the star of the show. Look for small, tender artichokes, and you may want to wear gloves when handling them, as they can stain your hands.

4 ounces fior di latte or buffalo mozzarella

½ lemon

1 cup ricotta

8 baby artichokes

¼ cup extra virgin olive oil

1 batch Impasto per la Pizza di Eataly (page 10) or Impasto per la Pizza Napoletana (page 24)

Flour for dusting work surface

½ cup Parmigiano Reggiano shavings

¼ cup minced parsley

CUT the mozzarella into 1-inch cubes. Set a sieve over a bowl and line the sieve with paper towels. Place the mozzarella in the towel-lined sieve and refrigerate for at least 2 hours and up to 8 hours to drain as much excess liquid as possible.

FINELY grate the lemon peel to make zest and combine with the ricotta. Set aside. Juice the lemon. Fill a large bowl with cold water and stir in the lemon juice. Remove any leaves from the stem of one of the artichokes and trim the end. Peel any tough skin from the outside of the stem. Cut off the tips of the artichokes leaves. Cut the artichoke in half the long way and then into quarters. With a paring knife, cut out and discard the choke. Drop the cut artichoke into the lemon water and repeat with remaining artichokes.

BRING a small saucepan of water to a boil and blanch the artichokes until soft enough to pierce easily with a knife, about 4 minutes. Drain, toss with 2 tablespoons oil, and set aside.

AT least 1 hour before you plan to bake the pizzas, place a rack with a baking stone on the second highest shelf (with no racks above it) and preheat the oven to its highest temperature. Most home ovens go up to at least 500°F; some may go higher. It is important to preheat the oven and the stone at length. If the highest heat you can achieve in your oven is on the broil setting, preheat the oven and stone to 500°F, then switch to the broiler setting before sliding in the pizza. (Alternatively, build a fire in a wood-burning oven and bring to 850°F to 900°F.)

DUST the top and sides of one of the risen dough rounds generously with flour. With a floured bench scraper, scrape the dough off of the surface and flip it over. Generously dust the dough with additional flour so that both sides are now floured.

STARTING in the center of the dough with your fingers, press down and away from you to flatten the dough. Flip the dough again, dusting with more flour as needed to keep it from sticking, and use the same method of pressing from the center outward until you have an even circle of dough 7 to 8 inches in diameter. Use the *schiaffo*, or slap, technique by taking your left hand facing upwards beneath the left side of the dough pulling outwards while your right hand slaps the top of the right side of the dough and pushes in the opposite direction while rotating. At this point try to use as little flour as possible without letting your dough stick to the work surface. Once your dough is about 10 inches in diameter and very thin, you are ready to add the toppings.

WITH a spoon, evenly space 4 tablespoons of the ricotta on the dough. Scatter on about one-quarter of the drained mozzarella. Scatter on 8 artichoke wedges. Drizzle with some of the remaining oil.

DUST a *pala*, or oven peel, with just enough flour to keep the dough from sticking and slide the pizza onto the peel. Once the pizza is on the peel you can gently stretch it a few more times so that it is 12 inches in diameter. Slide the pizza onto the pizza stone.

COOK, rotating the pizza twice, until the bottom is browned and the dough is blistered, 4 to 6 minutes. (It will cook in 1 to 1½ minutes in a wood-burning oven.) Meanwhile, repeat the process with the remaining dough.

AS soon as the pizza is baked, remove it from the oven and scatter the Parmigiano shavings on top, then garnish with the parsley.

SERVE immediately.

PIZZA MASSESE

SPICY SALAMI PIZZA

Makes 4 individual pizzas

Most salumi, or cold cuts, are placed on top of pizza after it is removed from the oven, but pork salami is sturdy enough to stand up to a few minutes of high heat. Just keep in mind that the salami is salty, so you will want to use a light hand when salting the tomato sauce.

8 ounces buffalo mozzarella

1¼ cups canned San Marzano tomatoes and their juice

½ teaspoon fine sea salt

1 batch Impasto per la Pizza di Eataly (page 10) or Impasto per la Pizza Napoletana (page 24)

Flour for dusting work surface

1 tablespoon extra virgin olive oil

6 ounces thinly sliced spicy salami

Fresh basil leaves

CUT the mozzarella into 1-inch cubes. Set a sieve over a bowl and line the sieve with paper towels. Place the mozzarella in the towel-lined sieve and refrigerate for at least 2 hours and up to 8 hours to drain as much excess liquid as possible.

AT least 1 hour before you plan to bake the pizzas, place a rack with a baking stone on the second highest shelf (with no racks above it) and preheat the oven to its highest temperature. Most home ovens go up to at least 500°F; some may go higher. It is important to preheat the oven and the stone at length. If the highest heat you can achieve in your oven is on the broil setting, preheat the oven and stone to 500°F, then switch to the broiler setting before sliding in the pizza. (Alternatively, build a fire in a wood-burning oven and bring to 850°F to 900°F.)

IN a small bowl combine the tomatoes and salt. Use your hands to crush the tomatoes and mix to combine.

DUST the top and sides of one of the risen dough rounds generously with flour. With a floured bench scraper, scrape the dough off of the surface and flip it over. Generously dust the dough with additional flour so that both sides are now floured.

STARTING in the center of the dough with your fingers, press down and away from you to flatten the dough. Flip the dough again, dusting with more flour as needed to keep it from sticking, and use the same method of pressing from the center outward until you have an even circle of dough 7 to 8 inches in diameter. Use the *schiaffo*, or slap, technique by taking your left hand facing upwards beneath the left side of the dough pulling outwards while your right hand slaps the top of the right side of the dough and pushes in the opposite direction while rotating. At this point try to use as little flour as possible without letting your dough stick to the work surface. Once your dough is about 10 inches in diameter and very thin, you are ready to add the toppings.

SPOON about one-quarter of the tomato mixture into the center of the pizza. Move the back of the spoon in a circular motion to spread the sauce evenly around the pizza, but leave the crust bare. Scatter on about one-quarter of the drained mozzarella and drizzle with oil.

DUST a *pala*, or oven peel, with just enough flour to keep the dough from sticking and slide the pizza onto the peel. Once the pizza is on the peel you can gently stretch it a few more times so that it is 12 inches in diameter. Slide the pizza onto the pizza stone.

COOK for 2 to 3 minutes, then scatter on one-quarter of the salami in a single layer. Continue to cook, rotating the pizza twice, until the bottom is browned and the dough is crisp, 4 to 6 minutes total. (It will cook in 1 to 1½ minutes in a wood-burning oven.) Meanwhile, repeat the process with the remaining dough.

GARNISH cooked pizza with basil.

SERVE immediately.

IMPASTO PER LA PIZZA AL PADELLINO

PAN PIZZA DOUGH

Makes dough for 4 individual pizzas

Torino's pizza al padellino (sometimes called pizza al tegamino) is an individual pan pizza with a thick crust. The outside of the crust turns crisp as it bakes in the oiled pan, but the interior is soft and almost fluffy. You will need four 8-inch round pans with 1- or 2-inch sides for this recipe. Cast-iron pans that develop a patina and retain heat effectively work especially well. At Eataly we sometimes serve the pizzas in their individual pans, but the pans are extremely hot, so at home you're better off taking them out of the pans. Since the dough is stretched in the pans and then sits for a little while, and since the use of a pan makes getting these pizzas in and out of the oven a snap, it can be fun to put out an array of options and have people top their own pizzas.

3½ cups buratto flour

1 cup plus 2 tablespoons bread flour

¼ teaspoon instant yeast

¼ cup plus 2 teaspoons extra virgin olive oil, plus more for oiling bowl

1 tablespoon fine sea salt

Flour for dusting bowl

IN the bowl of a stand mixer fitted with the dough hook, combine the flours, yeast, 2 teaspoons olive oil, salt, and 1⅓ cups water. Mix on lowest speed for 8 minutes.

RAISE to medium speed and mix for 12 minutes. Add ⅓ cup water in a thin stream and mix until combined, about 6 additional minutes.

LIGHTLY flour a large bowl. Transfer the dough to the bowl, cover, and set aside to proof at room temperature until doubled in size and puffy, about 3 hours.

TURN and fold the dough and gently shape it into a ball. Oil a large bowl. Place the dough in the oiled bowl, cover loosely, and allow to rise at room temperature until puffy, about 1 hour. Transfer the bowl to the refrigerator and refrigerate for 24 hours.

DIVIDE the dough into 4 equal portions. Shape each portion into a round ball with a smooth top. Cover loosely and let rest until the dough is room temperature, about 1 hour.

OIL four 8-inch round pans with 1 tablespoon olive oil each. Invert one ball of dough into one pan, smooth side down. Turn it over so that both sides are oiled. Gently, with your fingertips stretch the dough from the center outward to fill the pan. It will resist. When you have stretched it as much as you can without tearing it, let it rest at room temperature 10 to 15 minutes to relax the dough. Repeat with remaining dough and pans. Once the dough has rested, stretch each one entirely to the edge of its pan.

LET the dough rest in the pans at room temperature until it begins to puff, about 1 hour.

AT least 1 hour before you plan to bake the pizzas, place racks with baking stones or sheet pans on the upper third and lower third oven shelves and preheat the oven to its highest temperature. (Though the pizza is baked in a pan, the stone or sheet pans will help simulate a wood-burning oven.) Most home ovens go up to at least 500°F; some may go higher. (Alternatively, build a fire in a wood-burning oven and bring to 850°F to 900°F.)

SPREAD on tomato sauce and any other toppings that go on before baking (see below). Bake until crust is crisp and dark brown, 10 to 12 minutes. Remove pizzas from pans with a spatula and transfer to serving plates. Add any toppings that go on after baking.

SERVE immediately.

COME LA VUOI?

You can use almost any topping on pizza al padellino. Here are four of our favorite combinations (for 4 pizzas):

MARINARA
BEFORE BAKING: 3 cups canned, peeled tomatoes crushed by hand and seasoned with salt
AFTER BAKING: fresh basil leaves and a drizzle of extra virgin olive oil

MARGHERITA
BEFORE BAKING: 2 cups canned, peeled tomatoes crushed by hand and seasoned with salt and 8 ounces mozzarella, cut into cubes and drained
AFTER BAKING: fresh basil leaves and a drizzle of extra virgin olive oil

SOPPRESSATA
BEFORE BAKING: 2 cups canned, peeled tomatoes crushed by hand and seasoned with salt; arrange 32 thin slices (8 slices each) of soppressata to cover the tomato sauce, then top with 8 ounces mozzarella, cut into cubes and drained
AFTER BAKING: fresh basil leaves and a drizzle of extra virgin olive oil

ZUCCHINE E RICOTTA (opposite)
BEFORE BAKING: 1 thinly sliced medium zucchini tossed with salt and oil spread in a single layer to cover the surface
AFTER BAKING: ¾ cup ricotta dolloped onto the pizzas; sprinkle with minced fresh thyme and a few flakes of coarse sea salt and drizzle with extra virgin olive oil

TIELLA DI GAETA

THIN DOUBLE-CRUST PIZZA FROM GAETA

Makes one 11-inch pie, about 8 servings

This type of tiella (not to be confused with a Pugliese tiella, a casserole of rice, mussels, and potatoes) is a double-crust pizza baked in a pan (called, logically enough, a tiella). It hails from Gaeta, on the Tyrrhenian coast south of Roma, and was baked by local fishermen to use up the odds and ends of the catch. So in addition to Gaeta's famed black olives it is often stuffed with seafood, such as squid, octopus, cuttlefish, anchovies, or mussels, though it may also be filled with vegetables, such as escarole or eggplant. Bourbon King Ferdinand I apparently liked to wander among the commoners of Gaeta in disguise, munching on tiella.

2 pounds baby octopus, cleaned

3 medium tomatoes

¾ cup pitted Gaeta olives

¼ cup minced parsley

2 cloves garlic, minced

¼ cup extra virgin olive oil, plus more for brushing

¼ teaspoon salt

Salt to taste

Ground chili pepper to taste

1 ounce (about 2 tablespoons) lievito madre (see page 66)

4 cups 00 flour or unbleached all-purpose flour

FOR the filling, place the octopus in a pot. Add warm water just to cover and place over medium heat. Simmer until tender, about 20 minutes, then remove from the heat and let the octopus cool in the liquid. When the octopus is completely cool, drain and cut into small dice. Seed and dice the tomatoes and in a bowl combine the octopus, tomatoes, olives, parsley, and minced garlic. Drizzle on 1 tablespoon olive oil. Season to taste with salt and chili pepper and set aside while you prepare the dough. The filling can be prepared up to 2 days in advance and refrigerated.

IN a large bowl combine the lievito madre with 1 cup warm water. Break it up a little, then stir in the salt and the remaining 3 tablespoons oil. Add the flour a little at a time, stirring by hand to incorporate between additions, until you have a shaggy dough. Add water a little at a time if the dough feels dry. Transfer to a very lightly floured work surface and, using a bench scraper to move the dough around, knead until smooth and well-incorporated, about 10 minutes.

SHAPE the dough into a ball, drape a dishtowel over it, and let it rise at room temperature until puffy, 1 to 2 hours, but the time will vary depending on the strength of your lievito madre.

PREHEAT the oven to 350°F.

GENEROUSLY oil a 12-inch pizza pan or metal pie plate. Divide the dough into 2 equal portions. With a rolling pin, roll out one portion into a ¼-inch-thick disk, about 12 inches in diameter. If it retracts toward the center, let it rest for about 10 minutes then go back to it. Place the disk in the prepared pan. Spread the filling on top of the dough, leaving an empty ½-inch border around the perimeter. Roll out the second portion of dough in the same manner as the first and place it on top of the filling. Pinch the edges together to seal and crimp. (According to tradition, the border of the pie should sport *pizzocolle*, or wave-like fluting.) If the border seems excessively thick, trim off a little dough with a knife.

PRICK the top of the pie in several places with a fork, rub a generous amount of olive oil onto the top crust with your hand, and bake until golden, 30 to 35 minutes. Serve warm or at room temperature.

Variations

TIELLA DI POLPO COTTO NELLA SUA ACQUA: Use 2 pounds (about 2) octopus and the traditional method from Gaeta, where, as the saying goes, *il polpo si cucina nella sua stessa acqua*, or octopus cooks in its own juices. To cook the octopus, place it in a pot with a drizzle of olive oil and place over medium heat. An octopus gives off a lot of liquid as it cooks, about one third of its raw weight. Braise the octopus in its own juices until tender, about 45 minutes, then proceed as above.

TIELLA DI CALAMARI: You can use squid in place of the baby octopus. They cook in an instant, so keep a close eye on them and drain them as soon as they are done rather than allowing them to cool in the cooking liquid.

TIELLA DI SCAROLA: In place of the octopus mixture, blanch the leaves of 3 heads escarole, roughly chop, and sauté in olive oil with garlic, hot pepper, and ½ cup pitted Gaeta olives. If the escarole is tender, you can skip the blanching and add it to the pie raw. It will wilt as it bakes.

TIELLA DI MELANZANE: In place of the octopus mixture, slice 2 eggplant thinly the long way, brush with olive oil, and roast, panfry, or grill the slices until soft. Make a layer of eggplant slices on the bottom crust and spread about ½ cup canned tomatoes crushed by hand on the eggplant. Top with a layer of thin slices of mozzarella and sprinkle with 1 to 2 tablespoons grated Parmigiano Reggiano. Continue to make layers in this order until you have used up the eggplant.

TIELLA DI FORMAGGIO: Slice 2 yellow onions in half, then into half-moons, and sauté over low heat in a generous amount of olive oil until rich and golden. Let the onions cool, then combine them with 8 ounces fresh goat cheese, 2 beaten eggs, minced parsley, and minced fresh oregano. Season with salt and pepper and spread this filling on the bottom crust in place of the octopus mixture.

PIZZETTE

GOOD THINGS COME IN SMALL PACKAGES: this is true for pizza as well. A pizza in Italy is typically an individual serving, but there may be situations where you want to serve pizza as true finger food. Enter pizzette: round disks 2 to 3 inches in diameter that you can pop into your mouth in one or two bites. They're perfect with cocktails or as a snack.

YOU CAN MAKE PIZZETTE WITH ANY OF THE DOUGHS IN THIS CHAPTER simply by cutting the dough into smaller portions, shaping it into balls (each about the size of a golf ball), and stretching and topping them as desired. (See below for suggestions.) Each recipe will make approximately 30 bite-sized pizzas.

ITALIAN CAFÉS ALSO FREQUENTLY SELL PIZZETTE MADE WITH PUFF PASTRY. You can make your own (see page 70) or buy frozen puff pastry dough. Roll out the dough, then simply cut out circles with a round cookie cutter, top, transfer to parchment-lined sheet pans, and bake at 400°F until browned and puffed, 7 to 10 minutes.

WHICHEVER ROUTE YOU TAKE, BE JUDICIOUS WITH YOUR TOPPINGS. These small pizzas only have room for a dab of tomato sauce or a single slice of salami, and if the point of making pizzette is to allow your guests to eat them with their hands, you don't want sauce sluicing over the side. Here are a few ideas to get you started:

- A smear of crushed tomatoes and 1 to 2 cubes of mozzarella
- Mozzarella, gorgonzola, and 1 walnut half
- 1 thin slice of potato and a sprinkling of coarse salt
- Tomato sauce and 1 anchovy fillet
- Fontina and 1 small slice prosciutto crudo added after baking
- Olive oil, coarse salt, and rosemary (prick with a fork just before baking)

PASTA SFOGLIA PER PIZZETTE

PUFF PASTRY FOR PIZZETTE

Makes dough for 20 to 30 2- to 3-inch pizzette

Making puff pastry using the classic method is not difficult, but it is time-consuming because you need to keep refrigerating the dough in between folds so that the butter doesn't get too soft. Plan ahead. The instructions below are for completing two turns at a time, but if at any time the butter seems to be smearing (this tends to happen in warm weather, or even on a day when your oven has been on for a long time and is heating up the kitchen), rewrap the dough and refrigerate it until firm, about 30 minutes. Finished dough can be refrigerated for a few days or frozen for up to two weeks. You can also buy frozen sheets of puff pastry that are quite good. Be sure to select a puff pastry that uses only butter. Packaged puff pastry is sold in sheets, already rolled out and ready to be trimmed and baked. Let it thaw, but don't allow it to get warm. Remember always to roll puff pastry with the layers positioned horizontally.

1 stick plus 6 tablespoons unsalted butter

1½ cups bread flour

1 teaspoon salt

½ cup cold water

FIRST make a butter block. On your work surface on a piece of parchment paper, arrange the butter to form a rectangle. Fold the parchment paper over the top of the butter. With a rolling pin pound the butter to form a square, rotating it to keep the shape even. The goal is to have a single block of butter that is the same height throughout and flexible enough that it does not break when you bend it. The finished square should have sides about 4 to 5 inches long. Wrap the butter (you can use the parchment) and refrigerate while you make the dough and until it is chilled but still flexible, about 20 minutes.

FOR the dough, combine the flour, salt, and water in a large bowl. Knead into a smooth dough, then refrigerate the dough as well if the butter is not yet chilled. When you are ready to proceed, roll the dough into a rough square (about 9 inches per side) on a lightly floured work surface. Place the cold butter block in the center of the dough and fold the sides in over the butter, then fold the bottom of the dough up and the top down so that no butter is visible. Flip the package over, seam side down. (Lightly flour the work surface and the dough again if necessary.) Roll the dough to a rectangle about 12 by 8 inches. Fold the bottom up and the top down, like folding a letter. Turn the dough 1/4 turn so that it is now perpendicular to its original position (with the seam running down the middle toward you). Dust the dough and surface again if necessary and roll out the dough to a rectangle about ½ inch thick. Fold the bottom up and top down, wrap, and refrigerate for 30 minutes to 1 hour. Repeat this process a total of 3 times (for a total of 6 turns), refrigerating between every two folds or more often if necessary. By the time you are completing the final turns, the dough will be layered and smooth. Refrigerate the dough overnight.

PASTA SFOGLIA VELOCE
QUICK PUFF PASTRY

You can make a quicker version of puff pastry, also known as "rough puff," by cutting the butter into small pieces; it is slightly less flaky but still delicious. Have everything, even the flour, very cold when using this method. (You can freeze the butter and then grate it on the large holes of a four-sided grater.) Combine the flour and salt and work in about one-third of the cold butter the way you would for a pie crust, but not breaking down the butter too far—you should still see visible chunks. Then stir in the ice-cold water and form a rough dough. Refrigerate until firm, then roll out into a rectangle about 12 by 8 inches, scatter about half the remaining butter on the surface of the center of the rectangle, and fold the bottom up and the top down. Turn 1/4 turn so that the seam is running down the middle toward you and roll to ½ inch thick and fold again. Refrigerate, then place seam perpendicular to you, roll into a rectangle ½ inch thick, scatter on the remaining butter, and fold. Turn, roll, and fold two additional times without adding any more butter, then wrap and refrigerate for at least 3 hours before rolling and baking.

IL PIZZAIOLO

WORKING AS A PIZZAIOLO, or pizza maker, is a venerable career in Italy, where a pizzeria is always specifically designated as such (not a mere ristorante). It's a challenging job, too, as each guest orders their own individual pizza. A pizzaiolo in a successful pizzeria is constantly on the go—sliding pizzas smoothly into the oven, turning them, checking the bottoms, and pulling them out at just the right moment. Particularly in Napoli, a pizzaiolo will often develop a cult following and inspire fierce loyalty.

A great deal of training and cultivation of skill goes into mastering the craft of making pizza dough. In Italy, the toppings on a pizza are relatively spare; it is the dough that is the star of the dish. A pizzaiolo's hands are valuable and sensitive tools, and a feel for the dough is crucial. The annual Campionato Italiano di Pizza pits professional pizza makers from around the world against each other in timed competitions in several different categories, from classic to gluten free.

As for the professional pizzaioli of the world, for home bakers there is no substitute for experience—after you've made pizza a few times you'll begin to easily recognize the look of a well-risen dough and the feel of a perfectly shaped cornicione.

And one rule of the master pizzaiolo is easy to follow at home: Pizza is always served uncut in an Italian pizzeria, and diners are given knives and forks to slice it themselves. To eat your pizza properly, cut a triangular wedge with a knife and fork, then start eating from the pointed end of your slice. When the pizza has cooled and only a small portion of your slice is left, feel free to pick it up with your hands and eat it.

COSA BERE CON LA PIZZA?

WHETHER YOU'RE ENJOYING A PIZZA IN A PIZZERIA OR AT HOME, you'll want to drink something with it. Pizza and wine are made for one another, but not just any bottle can complement the iconic dish. After consulting our vino experts, we've narrowed down three things to consider when pairing these two Italian staples.

CONSIDER THE TOPPINGS

There is no one-wine-fits-all pizza rule. Instead, pairing wine and pizza together heavily depends on the toppings. Consider the ingredients and flavors first, then pair it with a wine that will either contrast or complement them. Here are a few guidelines for pairings:

TOMATO-BASED: Simple pizzas like a marinara or Margherita tend to go well with dry rosé wines and light reds.

WHITE PIZZA: Pizza bianca pairs well with white wines like Pinot Grigio, Falanghina, and even Prosecco.

MEATY: Meat-based pizzas, which are often strong in flavor, are balanced by medium-bodied, fruit-forward wines like Barbera, Barbaresco, or Sangiovese.

MUSHROOMS: The earthiness of a pizza con funghi (page 29) is supported by a savory, complex wine like a Chianti.

CHEESE: A cheese-forward pizza, like our cinque formaggi (page 49), is balanced by strong whites or bold reds like Aglianico, Cannonau di Sardegna, Montepulciano d'Abruzzo, or an oaky Sangiovese from Toscana.

GET BUBBLY

When in doubt, go for bubbles. Sparkling wines like Prosecco, Lambrusco, or a sparkling rosé will help cut through doughiness and act as a palate cleanser. Bubbly wines tend to go with a variety of toppings, making them a great choice to share with the whole table.

DRINK WHAT YOU LIKE

At the end of the day, there is no right or wrong answer when pairing pizza with wine. In fact, many Italians prefer beer or soda over wine when it comes to eating pizza. A birra bionda is a classic choice in an Italian pizzeria. Our number one rule: drink what you like!

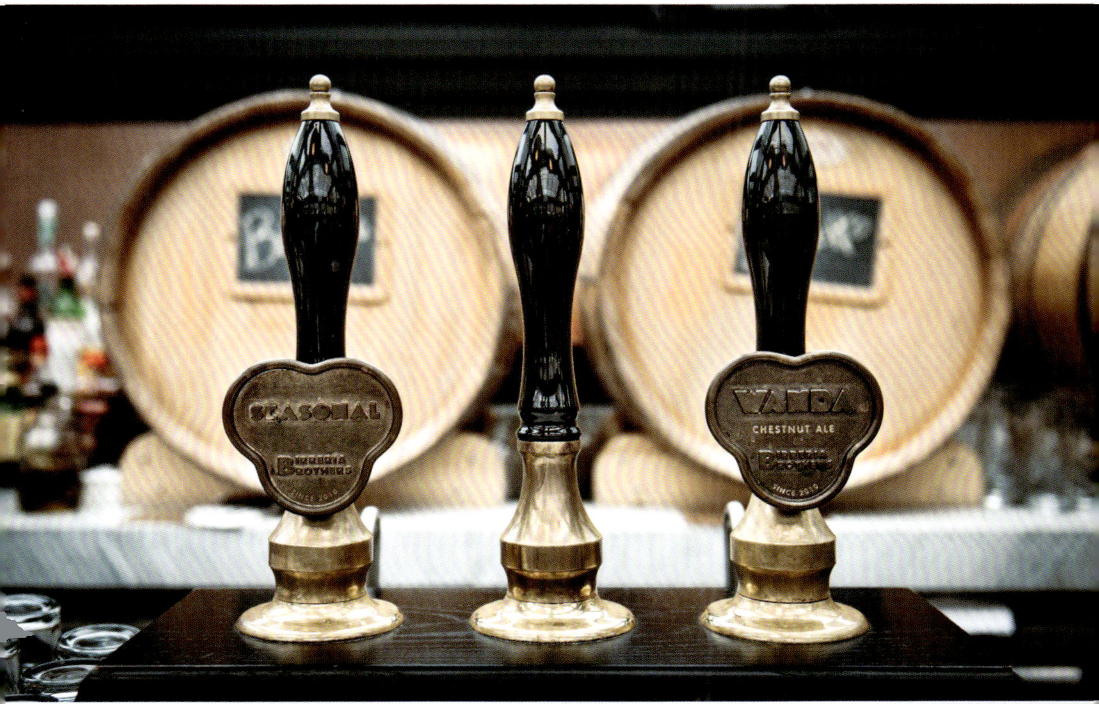
SEASONAL
WANDA
CHESTNUT ALE

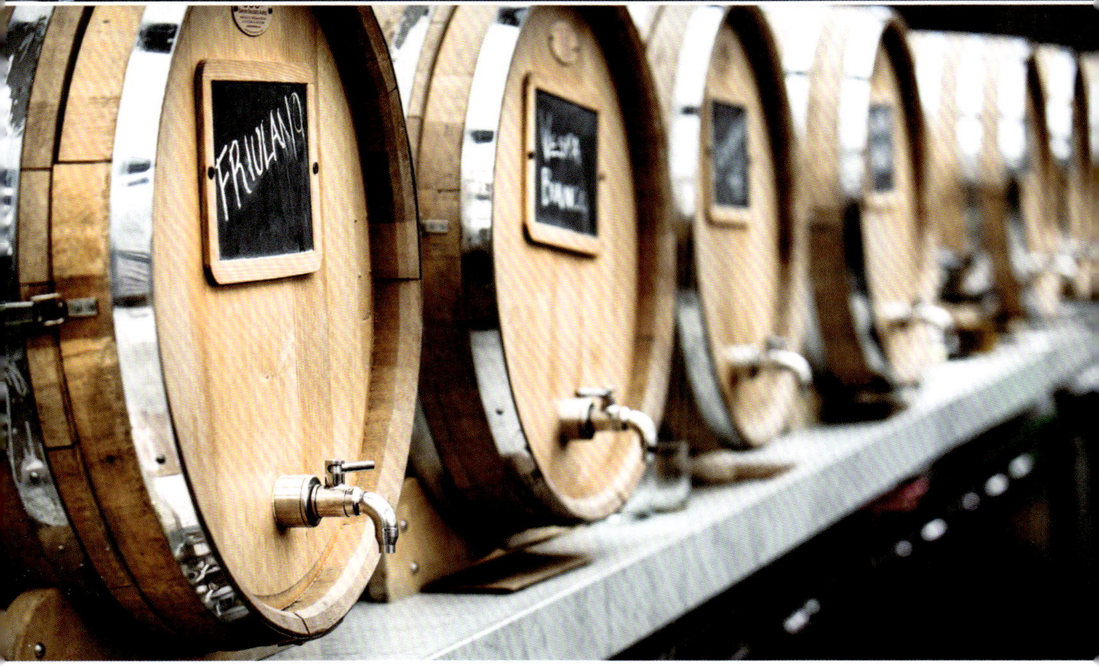

PIZZA AL TAGLIO E FOCACCIA

Warm, portable, versatile squares of pizza and focaccia are one of Italy's greatest gifts to the culinary world.

PIZZA AL TAGLIO

PIZZA AL TAGLIO, meaning pizza that is served by the slice and not as a whole pie, is Italy's premier street food. It comes in many guises and under many names: pizza romana, pizza alla pala, pizza al metro, pizza al trancio, and so on. It may be baked in a pan or directly on the floor of a pizza oven, and it can be thick, thin, or somewhere in between. Toppings range from the ultrasimple—a slick of olive oil, a few flakes of salt, perhaps a scattering of rosemary needles—to the complex. Sold in squares or rectangles (often by weight) wrapped in pieces of butcher's paper, a slice of this type of pizza is one of the world's most enjoyable open-air treats.

While strict traditions apply to pizza napoletana, when it comes to pizza al taglio, almost anything goes. There's been a boom in artisanal pizza-making in Italy in recent years, and Eataly is pleased to be a part of that story. Almost every Eataly store has a pizza counter with these tempting slabs on display.

Pizza is extremely popular, so if you're throwing a party and you want everyone to leave happy, from the youngest guest to the oldest, pizza is the obvious answer. But most home ovens will hold only one Neapolitan-style pizza at a time. The solution to a great pizza party is to make pizza alla pala.

Most of the work can be done in advance. Either purchase dough at Eataly or make your own using the recipe on page 80.

About 45 minutes before the party is scheduled to begin, stretch pizza dough into long ovals. (Or, if you prefer to bake them in pans, line a lightly oiled half-sheet pan with dough.)

About 1 hour before you're ready to bake the pizza, crank up your oven as high as it will go with pizza stones or overturned half-sheet pans on the shelves.

When you're ready to bake the pizza, transfer one oval of dough onto a wooden peel (the *pala* that gives this pizza its name), and scatter toppings onto the dough, or invite your guests to make their own.

When the pizza is topped, slide it into the oven. Bake until the crust is browned, about 20 to 25 minutes. After you remove the pizza, put on any fresh toppings, cut the pizza into squares or rectangles, and serve immediately.

Some of the most fun, casual gatherings we've hosted have been pizza parties, with a selection of different types of squares, some good beer and wine, and, in keeping with the theme, a sweet focaccia like the one on page 118 for dessert. The only limit is your imagination.

IMPASTO PER LA PIZZA ALLA PALA

PIZZA ALLA PALA DOUGH

Makes dough for 3 12 by 17-inch pizzass

This is the recipe for our pizza alla pala dough, which you can also purchase in Eataly stores. Pizza alla pala was created in Rome and features a slightly more dense—crispy on the outside, soft and airy on the inside—dough than pillowy pizza napoletana. It gets its name from the wooden peel, or *pala*, used to transfer these long ovals of dough in and out of the oven. Pizza alla pala actually came to be by happy accident. Bakers would slide long rectangular slaps of dough into their ovens to test the temperature. Eventually they began to top the cooked dough with fresh ingredients right on the pala. Therefore, in Rome you find pizza alla pala in bakeries, not in pizzerias. It is a true bakery pizza. If you prefer, you can instead press it into an oiled pan or place it in a parchment-lined pan. This recipe makes enough dough for three pizzas. If you prefer, you can make less, but the dough freezes beautifully. Pop a ball of dough into a freezer bag and freeze it, then thaw for a couple of hours before proceeding to bake it.

4 cups buratto flour

4 cups 00 flour or unbleached all-purpose flour

1 tablespoon plus 1½ teaspoons fine sea salt

1 tablespoon instant yeast

2 tablespoons extra virgin olive oil, plus more for bowls and drizzling

COMBINE the flours, salt, and yeast in a large bowl. In a separate bowl, whisk together 3 cups water and the 2 tablespoons olive oil, then add to the dry ingredients. Mix by hand until the mixture forms a crumbly dough, then transfer to a lightly floured work surface and knead until smooth and compact, 10 to 12 minutes. (Alternatively, knead the dough in a food processor fitted with the dough blade or a stand mixer fitted with the dough hook.)

TRANSFER the dough to a large bowl, cover the bowl, and let the dough rise at room temperature until doubled, about 2 hours.

REMOVE the dough and divide it into 3 equal pieces. Using your hands, roll the pieces of dough into round balls. Place them in an oiled bowl or tray (there shouldn't be too much room around them or they'll spread rather than rise). Cover with plastic or a dishtowel and let them rise at room temperature until very puffy, about 4 hours.

PIZZA ALLA PALA DI SALSICCIA, PEPERONI E CIPOLLA

SAUSAGE, PEPPER, AND ONION PIZZA ALLA PALA

Makes one 12 by 17-inch pizza, about 8 servings

Slabs of this hearty pizza disappear from behind the counter almost as fast as we can pull them from the oven at Eataly. Mixing different colored bell peppers makes this as attractive as it is tasty.

2 yellow bell peppers

1 red bell pepper

1 red onion

¼ cup extra virgin olive oil

2 cloves garlic, sliced

½ teaspoon crushed red pepper flakes

Fine sea salt to taste

8 ounces fresh pork sausage, cut into disks

1 cup crushed tomatoes

1 ball Impasto per la Pizza alla Pala (page 80), risen until puffy

Semolina flour for work surface and peel

2 tablespoons minced parsley

SEED and core the peppers and cut them into julienne. Thinly slice the onion into half-moons. In a large skillet, heat 1 tablespoon of the oil and sauté the peppers, onion, garlic, and red pepper flakes over medium heat until soft and slightly caramelized, about 10 minutes. Season with salt and set aside. In a separate skillet, heat 1 tablespoon oil and sauté the sausage until lightly browned, about 8 minutes. In a small bowl combine the crushed tomatoes with 1 tablespoon olive oil and season with salt.

PREHEAT the oven with a baking stone on the bottom shelf to 500°F.

PLACE the dough on a work surface lightly floured with semolina. If the top is overly sticky, very lightly flour with a little more semolina. To shape the dough, first gently press the sides of the dough with your fingertips to flatten, working from top to bottom. Slide your fingertips under the edges of the dough and gently pull it sideways into a rectangular shape. Press down the center of the dough with your fingertips, working from top to bottom, to lengthen. If the dough resists or snaps back, let it sit for a few minutes. After it rests briefly, it should be easier to stretch.

TRANSFER the dough to a pizza peel lightly floured with semolina. Gently stretch the dough so that it is about 17 inches long and 12 inches wide, and straighten the sides so that it is a rough rectangle with rounded corners. Jiggle to be sure the dough isn't sticking to the peel. If it is, run a large offset spatula underneath to detach it. (While in pizzerias these pizzas are usual baked

perpendicular to the oven door, you will likely need to turn it sideways so it fits on your baking stone.)

SPREAD the tomato mixture over the surface of the dough. Spread on the pepper and onion mixture evenly. Sprinkle on the cooked sausage. Slide the pizza into the oven and bake until golden and crisp on the bottom but still soft in the center, about 15 minutes. Slide the pizza onto a cutting board. Sprinkle on the parsley and drizzle with the remaining 1 tablespoon olive oil. Cut in half lengthwise and then across into 4 strips for a total of 8 slices each. Serve immediately.

TOPPINGS

THERE ARE THREE TYPES OF TOPPINGS FOR PIZZA ALLA PALA: those that are scattered onto the dough raw and baked in the heat of the oven, those that are cooked in advance and reheated in the oven, and those that are served fresh. Creating combinations is up to you, but we like to serve at least one classic Margherita-style pizza at any gathering, and we aim for about half of the pizzas we serve to be vegetarian. You can either have guests scatter on their own toppings or make the decision for them.

TOPPINGS THAT BAKE IN THE OVEN

Crushed tomatoes mixed with olive oil and seasoned with salt

Thinly sliced zucchini

Thinly sliced red or yellow onions

Zucchini flowers

Thinly sliced mushrooms

Diced pancetta

TOPPINGS COOKED IN ADVANCE

Boiled potatoes, sliced or crushed

Slices of grilled eggplant

Porchetta or other roasted pork, thinly sliced

Sautéed greens

Sliced sausage

Caramelized onions

Sautéed bell peppers

Roasted Brussels sprouts

Roasted winter squash

TOPPINGS SERVED FRESH

Prosciutto and other thinly sliced cured meats

Arugula

Ricotta

Halved cherry tomatoes

Very ripe fresh figs, halved

Canned tuna, drained and flaked

Burrata

Stracciatella

Sliced fresh heirloom tomatoes

Anchovy fillets

Olives

Smoked salmon

Grated Parmigiano Reggiano and Grana Padano

Minced fresh herbs

TOPPING COMBINATIONS

YOU COULD MIX AND MATCH THE TOPPINGS ABOVE ALMOST ENDLESSLY, but here are a few of the combinations (some traditional and some not) that we offer at Eataly:

PIZZA ALLA PALA BIANCA (WHITE PIZZA ALLA PALA): A white pizza alla pala topped simply with 2 tablespoons of olive oil and a sprinkling of salt before baking is a great quick substitute for bread and can be split horizontally for sandwiches. It can also be cut into squares and then topped with an endless array of uncooked toppings, such as prosciutto crudo and burrata.

PIZZA ALLA PALA BURRATA E POMODORO (PIZZA ALLA PALA WITH BURRATA AND TOMATOES): This rich and delicious pizza is made by spreading crushed tomatoes mixed with olive oil and salt over the base. Bake and allow to cool slightly. Slice and top each slice with a medium ball of burrata. Scatter halved cherry tomatoes around the cheese and garnish with basil. Drizzle with olive oil and serve.

PIZZA ALLA PALA TRICOLORE (THREE-COLOR PIZZA ALLA PALA): This pizza displays the colors of the Italian flag. Spread crushed tomatoes mixed with olive oil and salt over the base. Bake, then top with shreds of stracciatella. Arrange halved cherry tomatoes on the cheese, and sprinkle arugula over the top. Drizzle with olive oil.

PIZZA ALLA PALA BACON E UOVO (BACON AND EGG PIZZA ALLA PALA): Okay, bacon and eggs aren't Italian, but who doesn't love this classic American combination? Brush the dough with olive oil and sprinkle with salt. Cook the pizza for 3 minutes. The dough will still be soft. Transfer the pizza to a parchment-lined half-sheet pan and use your fist to make 8 evenly spaced indentations (2 rows of 4) in the dough. Use bacon strips to construct a square frame around each indentation, but leave the indentations exposed. Return the pan to the oven and bake until the bacon begins to brown but is still a little pliable, about 5 minutes. Crack 1 egg in each indentation. Return to the oven and bake until the bacon is browned and the eggs are beginning to set, about 4 minutes. Sprinkle shredded provolone over the surface and bake until cheese is melted, bacon is crisp, and eggs are set, about 4 additional minutes. Season with freshly ground black pepper and drizzle with olive oil.

PIZZA ALLA PALA AL SALMONE (SALMON PIZZA ALLA PALA): Another untraditional but tasty favorite. Brush the dough with olive oil and sprinkle with salt. Bake until golden and crisp on the bottom but still soft in the center, about 15 minutes. Slide the pizza onto a cutting board. Cut into slices. Top each slice with a couple of slices of smoked salmon and a small piece of stracciatella. Finely grate the zest of a lemon over the entire pizza. Sprinkle on some arugula and drizzle with olive oil.

PIZZA ALLA PALA CAVOLETTI E PANCETTA (BRUSSELS SPROUTS AND PANCETTA PIZZA ALLA PALA): Sprinkle chopped mozzarella over the dough. Top with roasted Brussels sprouts separated into individual leaves. Sprinkle on diced pancetta and additional mozzarella. Bake until golden, about 15 minutes. Sprinkle on grated Parmigiano and drizzle with olive oil. This is also great with ribbons of roasted or sautéed kale in place of the Brussels sprouts.

PIZZA ALLA PALA ALLA ZUCCA (SQUASH PIZZA ALLA PALA): Sprinkle chopped mozzarella over the dough. Top with diced roasted winter squash and additional mozzarella. Bake until golden, about 15 minutes. Sprinkle with grated Parmigiano, minced chives, and a drizzle of olive oil.

PIZZA ALLA PALA CAROTE E RICOTTA (PIZZA ALLA PALA WITH CARROTS AND RICOTTA): Sprinkle chopped mozzarella over the dough and bake until golden, about 15 minutes. Spread ricotta over the surface of the dough and top with roasted carrots (we like to use a mix of heirloom carrots for color and flavor), thin slices of radish, and fresh thyme leaves. Drizzle with olive oil.

PIZZA ALLA PALA LIMONE E RICOTTA (LEMON RICOTTA PIZZA ALLA PALA): Tart, sweet, and salty—this pizza is always a winner. Thinly slice 1 lemon (preferably using a mandoline), toss with salt, then arrange the slices on top of the dough. Top with cubes of mozzarella, drizzle with olive oil, and bake until dough is golden, about 15 minutes. Drop dollops of ricotta on top of the dough. Drizzle with honey, and sprinkle with flaky sea salt and fresh thyme. Drizzle with a bit more olive oil.

L'IMPASTATURA

WHAT'S THE PURPOSE OF KNEADING?

When you knead you are both incorporating air into the dough and developing the gluten in the flour to create a strong structure. (For more about flour, see page 18.) You can test gluten development by doing the windowpane test. Pull off a chunk of dough and stretch it. When gluten is well-developed, it will form a thin sheet called a gluten window; when gluten is underdeveloped, it will snap. But kneading isn't the only source of gluten development. Gluten also develops as the dough rests, so if you ever feel you have under-kneaded your dough, give it a slightly longer time to rest than the recipe dictates. In any case, the times provided in recipes are always flexible—rely on your hands and your eyes rather than slavishly following the timing provided. While kneading develops gluten, it's the final stretching and shaping of the dough that determines the shape and crumb after baking.

Don't be tempted to douse your dough or work surface with flour in order to make it easy to handle. Use a bench scraper to manipulate very wet doughs (with a high proportion of water to flour). One of the most magical things about kneading is the effect it has. Your dough will be shaggy and rough-looking at the start, but as you knead, it will grow smoother and more tender. Even the stickiest dough is somewhat tamed by kneading.

We find kneading by hand very soothing, but some days you simply don't have the time or energy for kneading (at Eataly as as well in other commercial bakeries, of course, we're working with such significant volumes of dough that we use a large mixer for kneading). Both a food processor and a stand mixer do a good job of kneading dough.

FOR A FOOD PROCESSOR:

Fit the food processor with the dough blade, which is usually made of plastic. Place the dry ingredients in the bowl and pulse a few times to combine. With the machine running, add the liquid ingredients through the tube. Process until the dough forms a ball, then process for about 45 additional seconds.

FOR A STAND MIXER:

Fit the mixer with the dough hook. Mix on the second-lowest speed until the dough forms a ball and cleans the sides of the bowl, about 2 minutes. If the dough begins to climb the hook attachment, it has been kneaded long enough.

THE PROCESS OF KNEADING DOUGH IS OFTEN SHROUDED IN MYSTERY, BUT IT'S REALLY QUITE SIMPLE:

1. Place the dough on a surface (preferably wooden) that is about level with your hips. Often you will be instructed to flour the work surface lightly—this means adding flour in small pinches. Never coat the surface heavily.

2. Push the dough down and away from you with the heels of your hands.

3. Fold the dough over toward you, turn it 45 degrees, and again push the dough down and away from you with the heels of your hands.

4. Continue this process of pushing, folding, and turning until the dough is smooth and elastic. If you are a practiced kneader, for most recipes this will take about 8 minutes when done by hand.

FOCACCIA GENOVESE

FOCACCIA WITH ROSEMARY AND SALT

Makes one 12 by 17-inch focaccia

Fresh focaccia is a joy. Just before baking, you lavish a generous amount of salamoia on top of the dimpled dough. We use a combination of lievito madre and instant yeast for our focaccia at Eataly. You can leave out the lievito madre if you like and increase the amount of yeast to 1 teaspoon. Focaccia is also wonderful for sandwiches.

1¾ cups 00 flour or unbleached all-purpose flour

1¾ cups bread flour

1 ounce (about 2 tablespoons) lievito madre (see page 16)

1 tablespoon plus ¼ teaspoon fine sea salt

½ teaspoon instant yeast

3 tablespoons plus 1 teaspoon extra virgin olive oil, plus more for bowl and pan

1 teaspoon coarse sea salt

1 tablespoon minced fresh rosemary leaves

IN a bowl, combine the flours with 1⅓ cups lukewarm water and stir to combine. Add the lievito madre (dissolved in a little more water if it is very stiff) and stir to combine.

SPRINKLE on 1 tablespoon of the fine sea salt and the yeast. Drizzle on 1 tablespoon plus 1 teaspoon of the olive oil. Turn the dough out onto a lightly floured work surface and knead until thoroughly combined and soft, about 10 minutes. (Alternatively, knead the dough in a food processor fitted with the dough blade or a stand mixer fitted with the dough hook.)

LIGHTLY oil a bowl, turn the dough into the bowl, cover tightly, and set aside to rise at room temperature until doubled in size, about 1½ hours.

GENEROUSLY oil a half-sheet pan and turn the dough onto it. With your fingertips, begin to stretch the dough (see page 92) to fill the pan. It will most likely spring back and resist. Do not tear the dough. If the dough does resist, cover loosely and set aside for up to 1 hour until it stops resisting. Stretch the dough so that it fills the pan. Again, if it stretches somewhat but then springs back into the middle, set the dough aside and wait. By the third try, the dough should relax enough that you can stretch it to fill the pan.

WHEN the dough fills the pan, set it aside to rest at room temperature for 30 minutes. If you are using a baking stone, place it on the lowest rack of the oven. Remove the other racks. Preheat the oven to 425°F.

TO make the salamoia, in a small bowl, for 1 minute vigorously whisk together the remaining 2 tablespoons olive oil with 1 tablespoon water and the remaining ¼ teaspoon salt until emulsified. Immediately pour the mixture all over the focaccia. Press with your fingertips to make dimples about 1 inch apart across the entire surface of the focaccia. Sprinkle on the coarse salt and rosemary.

BAKE, turning front to back about halfway through, on the bottom rack (on the stone if using) until the top of the focaccia is golden and the bottom is a little darker and crisp, about 15 minutes. Serve hot or at room temperature.

Variations

FOCACCIA PER PANINI (SANDWICH FOCACCIA): Omit the rosemary and coarse sea salt.

FOCACCIA ALLA CIPOLLA (ONION FOCACCIA): Thinly slice or shred red onions, toss with olive oil, salt, and rosemary, and spread on top of the focaccia in place of the salamoia.

FOCACCIA ALLE ZUCCHINE (ZUCCHINI FOCACCIA): Thinly slice 1 large zucchini and 1 large yellow summer squash and toss with a few tablespoons extra virgin olive oil, salt and pepper, and grated grana cheese, such as Parmigiano Reggiano. Omit salamoia and bake for 8 minutes, then spread about ½ cup ricotta on top of the focaccia, sprinkle on the zucchini, and bake until zucchini is lightly browned and focaccia is golden, about 8 additional minutes. Tear fresh basil leaves over the baked focaccia.

HOW TO FORM FOCACCIA

FOCACCIA COMES BY ITS DIMPLED SURFACE HONESTLY—as you're pressing the dough into the pan, you create those little indentations that are perfect for capturing little pools of oil and salt.

1. Place the focaccia dough on an oiled pan.

2. Press lightly with your fingertips while pushing outward on the dough.

3. If the dough resists, let it sit for at least 10 minutes or up to 1 hour. When you come back to it, the gluten will have relaxed and the dough will easily stretch to fit the pan.

FOCACCIA DI VOLTRI

THIN FOCACCIA FROM VOLTRI

Makes one 12 by 17-inch focaccia, about 8 servings

Today Voltri is a neighborhood in the greater Genova area, though it once was a separate village. Voltri's focaccia is thin, and it rises and bakes on surfaces sprinkled with cornmeal, giving it a satisfying crunch. In the bakeries in Voltri, this type of focaccia is usually thinned as it goes into the oven: bakers allow it to catch slightly on the peel so that as they pull the peel away the dough is stretched (rather than being pressed into the pan like focaccia Genovese (page 90). The recipe below achieves the same effect by having you pull it thin in a pan. This dough is a little sticky, but don't be tempted to douse it in flour to make it easier to handle—just use a bench scraper whenever needed.

1¾ cups bread flour, plus more for work surface

1 teaspoon fine sea salt

1 teaspoon sugar

½ teaspoon instant yeast

¼ cup extra virgin olive oil

¼ cup polenta or other stoneground cornmeal

IN a large bowl combine the bread flour, salt, sugar, and yeast. Add ¾ cup warm water and stir to combine into a shaggy dough. Knead on an unfloured work surface until the mixture is smooth and well-combined, 8 to 10 minutes.

RETURN the dough to the bowl and drizzle in 2 tablespoons of the oil a little at a time, kneading to incorporate between additions. Knead for 5 additional minutes. (It is easiest to incorporate the oil with the dough in the bowl, but once it is incorporated you may find it easier to knead on an unfloured work surface.) Pull off a bit of dough and check the gluten development by stretching the dough. It should form a window. If instead the dough breaks, continue kneading for 3 to 4 minutes, then check again. (Alternatively, knead the dough in a food processor fitted with the dough blade or a stand mixer fitted with the dough hook.)

PLACE the dough on a clean, lightly floured surface and gently shape into a rectangle about 6 by 3 inches. Cover with a damp dishtowel and allow to rest for 15 minutes. Gently flatten the dough into a rectangle about 8 by 6 inches. Using a dough scraper to detach it from the surface if necessary, fold it down from the top and up from the bottom, like a business letter. Fold in the left and right sides. Turn it over so the smooth side is facing up.

SPRINKLE a half-sheet pan or a separate area of your work surface with about 2 tablespoons cornmeal. With a rolling pin, roll the dough into a ¾- to 1-inch thick rectangle, about 8 by 6 inches. Transfer the rectangle of dough to the cornmeal-coated prepared pan or work surface. Cover the dough with plastic wrap, and arrange a dishtowel on top of the plastic wrap. Allow to rise at room temperature for 2 hours, by which point it should be quite puffy and bubbly.

ARRANGE a rack on the lowest level of the oven and preheat to 475°F.

SPRINKLE a (second) half-sheet pan with the remaining cornmeal. Transfer the rectangle of dough to the second pan. (You can use a large spatula or 2 dough scrapers to lift it.) Drizzle the remaining 2 tablespoons olive oil onto the dough. Use your fingertips to dimple the dough all over and distribute the oil over the surface. When the dough is dimpled and oiled, grasp one end with one hand, lift it off the pan slightly, and pull it toward the edge of the pan to stretch it. Don't worry if it stretches unevenly, but do try to lift the dough so that it stretches from the center. Turn the pan and repeat on each side of the dough until it fills the pan. (It may resist a little at first.)

BAKE until golden, 8 to 10 minutes.

SERVE warm.

A FOCACCIA BY ANY OTHER NAME

PAN BREADS SIMILAR TO FOCACCIA ARE BAKED ALL OVER ITALY. The thickness of the dough, the toppings, and the specific methods developed over centuries are what differentiate these breads from each other. Below is a small sampling of local types of focaccia.

SARDENAIRA Sardenaira, also known as piscialandrea, is the San Remo-native cousin to Nice's pissaladière: focaccia dough topped with tomatoes, garlic, anchovies, and olives. This is a popular snack on the region's beaches.

PITTA CHINA Calabrese pitta china (*china* is dialect for "stuffed") is a double-crust focaccia that can be filled with any number of ingredients, including all kinds of cured meats and cheese, anchovies, canned tuna, capers, eggplant, or tomatoes. We're partial to the version with spicy salami and whole hard-boiled eggs. The crust may be thick or thin. There are several other forms of pitta in Calabria, including a ring-shaped loaf of bread that can be cut in half horizontally and filled, then sliced up for curved sandwiches, and pitta 'mpigliata, a dessert made by spreading a raisin and nut filling on dough, rolling it up jelly-roll style, and slicing it into buns that are then turned on their side and baked.

FOCACCIA MESSINESE Messina is located on the northeast coast of Sicilia, right across from mainland Italy. The city is known for its ornate Gothic churches and, of course, for its food. Its signature focaccia is topped with endive and anchovies, and mild tuma cheese, which is usually made from sheep's milk. The dough is made with lard rather than olive oil. It uses a small amount of yeast and is given a long, slow rise to develop flavor.

SFINCIONE The sfincione of Sicilia is less chewy than northern types of focaccia. Indeed, its name comes from the Greek word for "sponge," a nod to its fluffy texture. The dough is not pressed flat in the pan but is left thick and tall. All of the island's traditional ingredients—olives, anchovies, and more—can be found atop sfincione; in Palermo it is often adorned with anchovies and a layer of crispy breadcrumbs.

focaccia di recco

focaccia with sausage, onion, and peppers

focaccia with parmacotto and mozzarella

focaccia with tomato and mozzarella

focaccia with zucchini and squash *focaccia with tomato and oregano*

focaccia genovese *focaccia with onions*

OLIO D'OLIVA

OLIVES ARE A FRUIT, and olive oil is a fresh fruit juice—a pretty delicious one. Every year in the fall, olives are harvested across Italy. Then the olives are pressed using a time-honored process. (Like wine, olive oil has a vintage—the harvest date should appear on the bottle.) Extra virgin olive oil is the highest quality—the term indicates that an oil is from the first pressing, which means it's lower in acidity.

Olive oil is a key ingredient in focaccia. One of the identifying characteristics of an authentic focaccia is the slick of oil on the top that forms delicious pools in the dimples on the surface of the dough. This is created by topping the focaccia with salamoia, or brine, which is basically two parts oil to one part water whisked together with salt and then poured over the top of the focaccia before it goes into the oven. The water evaporates as the focaccia bakes, leaving the oil atop a crispy surface that is browned—darkly in some spots and lightly golden in others.

Fine olive oil is expensive, but for good reason—many of the olives for high-quality oils are handpicked and then cold-pressed within hours of the harvest. This results in an oil that captures the taste and aroma of the fruit—an oil that truly tastes of olives. Unless you're making truffle focaccia, all the other ingredients you'll use are incredibly inexpensive. Splurge on the olive oil.

Additionally, olive oil is like wine, in the sense that you shouldn't cook with an olive oil you wouldn't happily consume in its raw state. We've seen the advice over the years to cook with lesser quality olive oil, but as Italians, we shudder at that idea. Locate an olive oil that you enjoy—whether it be grassy, mild, peppery, or sweet—and stock up on it. But don't buy more than you can use over the course of a few months and expect it to last infinitely. Time, light, heat, and air are the enemies of olive oil. We store our bottles away from the windows in our stores, and you should do the same at home—and don't store the oil near your stove or other sources of heat, either. Treat your olive oil well and you will be repaid many times over.

ANATOMY OF AN OLIVE OIL BOTTLE

HARVEST DATE A bottle of olive oil should bear a *harvest date;* the freshest oils are best. Unlike wine, olive oil does not need to be aged.

CULTIVAR High-quality olive oil always indicates the type of olives, or *cultivar,* used.

REGION OF ORIGIN High-quality Italian olive oil will name the *region of origin* and not just say "Product of Italy." Bottles labeled with the country in general may contain oil that was simply bottled in Italy but came from olives grown elsewhere.

HOW TO TASTE OLIVE OIL

OLIVE OIL TASTING IS SIMILAR TO WINE TASTING, and just like wines, olive oils have a very wide variety of tastes and aromas. A tasting can both sharpen your palate and allow you to identify what kind of oil you prefer. Stage a home tasting of at least three and no more than five oils as a prelude to your next dinner party—it's a fun way to get the evening started and pique both appetites and curiosity.

1. Pour a tablespoon or two of olive oil into a stemless wineglass. (The pros use special blue glasses that are intended to disguise the color of the oil, which says little about the flavor but might unconsciously affect judgment.)

2. Cup the glass in your hands and swirl the oil gently to release aromas.

3. Stick your nose in the glass and inhale deeply.

4. Slurp a mouthful of oil while inhaling noisily, just as your mother taught you not to eat soup. Drawing air in heightens the flavor. Then breathe out through your nose.

5. Swallow while concentrating on the flavor.

6. Between oils, cleanse your palate with a thin slice of Granny Smith apple or a cube of plain bread.

OLIVE OIL VOCABULARY

The three basic categories to consider for olive oil are fruitiness, pungency, and bitterness. Here are some other flavors and qualities you may discern in olive oil:

almond	apple	artichoke	banana	buttery	cherry
creamy	floral	grassy	green tomato	herbaceous	nutty
peppery	pine	pine nuts	stone fruit	sweet	

Roi Cru Riva Gianca *Mandranova Nocellara* *Frantoio Franci Montenero d'Orcia*

FOCACCIA DI RECCO

CHEESE-STUFFED FOCACCIA FROM RECCO

Makes one 12- to 14-inch focaccia, about 8 wedges

Recco is a town on the Ligurian coastline known for this unusual version of focaccia, made by stretching an unyeasted dough very thin—almost like strudel dough—and then filling it with soft cow's milk cheese. The Saracens attacked Recco in the thirteenth century and its citizens fled to the hills, where they made do with the few provisions they managed to bring with them, namely olive oil, flour, and cheese. The resulting bread is now the town's calling card, and Recco holds a festival dedicated to it every year in May. In Recco the focaccia is always baked in a very large copper pan; this recipe has been cut down to be made in a standard 12- to 14-inch round pan, but of course if you have a copper pan (which excels at conducting heat) you should use it. The cheese makes this rather rich, but one wedge is a lovely appetizer.

1¾ cups 00 flour or unbleached all-purpose flour, plus more for the work surface

1 teaspoon fine sea salt

¼ cup extra virgin olive oil, plus more for bowl, pan, and brushing

8 ounces stracchino

COMBINE the flour and salt in a large bowl. In a separate bowl, whisk together ½ cup water and the ¼ cup olive oil, then add to the dry ingredients. Mix by hand until the mixture forms a crumbly dough, then transfer to a lightly floured work surface and knead until smooth and compact, 10 to 12 minutes. (Alternatively, knead the dough in a food processor fitted with the dough blade or a stand mixer fitted with the dough hook.)

SHAPE the dough into a ball, wrap in plastic or a damp dishtowel, and set aside to rest at room temperature for 1 hour. Do not skimp on the resting time.

PLACE a baking stone on the bottom shelf of the oven and preheat to 550°F (or as hot as your oven will go).

GENEROUSLY oil a 12- to 14-inch round pan and set aside.

LIGHTLY flour the work surface. Divide the dough into two pieces, one slightly larger than the other. Roll out the larger piece of dough to a very thin disk. (If the dough resists, set it aside for a few minutes and then go

back to it.) When you have finished rolling the dough, gently slide your fists under the dough and stretch it. It should be so thin that it is almost transparent and a little wider in diameter than your pan. Don't worry if the dough tears as you do this—just pinch it together.

LINE the prepared pan with this first disk of dough. Pinch off pieces of the cheese and scatter the pieces over the dough. (The cheese is soft, but don't try to spread it—you'll just end up tearing the dough beneath it.)

ROLL and stretch the second piece of dough into a disk just as you did the first. Arrange the disk on top of the cheese. Seal the edges all around the perimeter, then use a rolling pin to cut off any excess dough. (You can roll this dough into breadsticks and bake them.) Seal around the edge again.

BRUSH the top of the focaccia with a generous amount of olive oil. Pulling with your fingers, create 4 or 5 tears in the top layer of dough.

BAKE on the baking stone until golden and puffed, 10 to 12 minutes. Slide the focaccia from the pan onto a cutting board.

SERVE immediately.

ATTREZZI E UTENSILI

BENCH SCRAPER: A bench scraper is a rectangular metal blade attached to a handle. Use it to detach dough from the work surface and to handle particularly sticky doughs. (If you use a bench scraper, you won't need to add large amounts of flour to handle a wet dough, which can weigh it down.)

PEEL: A peel, or *pala*, is a wooden or metal pallet with a long handle that is used to transfer dough in and out of the oven with a quick push. Always slightly jiggle the peel to make sure your dough is not sticking to it before sliding the dough onto a baking stone. If it does seem to be sticking, run a long offset spatula between the dough and the peel to separate it.

BAKING STONE: A baking stone, sometimes labeled a pizza stone or bread stone, is used in a home oven to recreate the stone floor of a wood-burning oven, which retains heat masterfully. The material may be ceramic, stone, or steel, all of which conduct heat well—the latter being a recent addition to the market. Always place the stone in the oven while the oven is preheating, and let it cool down in the oven as well. To clean a stone, usually you only need to wipe off any excess flour, but if a pizza stone gets dirty, scrub it with a damp towel and allow it to dry completely before using it again. If you don't have a stone, you can approximate one by overturning a sheet pan on an oven rack.

PANS: Many types of pizza, such as pizza napoletana, bake directly on a pizza stone, but other types, such as focaccia, are baked in a pan. Round pizza pans have a very low rim; round cake pans (used for the pizza al padellino on page 64) have 1- or 2-inch sides. Pans may be made of cast-iron, aluminum, or stainless steel. Focaccia di Recco (page 101) is traditionally made in a copper pan.

CUTTERS: A wheel cutter, or mezzaluna, makes quick work of slicing a pizza into squares or wedges.

YOUR HANDS: Making pizza and bread typically doesn't require as much finesse as crafting delicate pastries. You can (and should) use your hands for about 90 percent of the related tasks, including kneading, shaping dough, spreading dough into a pan, and even brushing the top of a crust with olive oil. When you've got a little practice under your belt, you'll know from touch when a pizza dough is ready and when rolls have risen to just the right stage for baking.

FOCACCIA BARESE

BARI-STYLE FOCACCIA WITH TOMATOES, OLIVES, AND OREGANO

Makes one 9-inch round focaccia, about 8 servings

The Puglia region and its capital city, Bari, have their own form of focaccia. (The word focaccia derives from the Latin *focus*, or hearth.) It is thicker than the type from Genova and Liguria and usually baked in a round pan, and the dough incorporates semolina flour (the signature ingredient in Puglia's famed orecchiette pasta and its pane di Altamura). Some people knead a mashed boiled potato into the dough for an especially tender interior. The traditional toppings are tomatoes and olives, and, of course, a generous amount of olive oil to create a crunchy crust that contrasts delightfully with the soft crumb.

1 cup rimacinata semolina flour

1¾ cups 00 flour or unbleached all-purpose flour, plus more for work surface

1 teaspoon instant yeast

1 teaspoon fine sea salt

¼ cup plus 2 tablespoons extra virgin olive oil

¼ teaspoon coarse sea salt

5 to 6 roma tomatoes

½ cup pitted Taggiasca olives

1 teaspoon dried oregano

IN a large bowl combine the flours, yeast, and salt. Add 1 cup warm water and stir to combine. Add 2 tablespoons of the olive oil and stir until well combined, then transfer to a lightly floured work surface and knead until smooth and compact, about 8 minutes. (Alternatively, knead the dough in a food processor fitted with the dough blade or a stand mixer fitted with the dough hook.)

OIL a bowl with 1 tablespoon olive oil. Shape the dough into a ball, place in the oiled bowl, then turn it over so that it is oiled on all sides. Cover the bowl and set aside to rise at room temperature until quite puffy, about 2 hours.

USE 1 tablespoon olive oil to oil a 9-inch round pan with 2-inch sides. Place the dough in the pan and gently press it with your fingertips to fill the pan. If the dough resists, set it aside to rest briefly, then try again.

FOR the salamoia, in a small bowl, briskly whisk together the remaining 2 tablespoons olive oil with 1 tablespoon water and the coarse salt for 1 minute to emulsify. Immediately pour the mixture over the dough. Dimple with your fingertips. Crush the tomatoes by hand, letting the pieces and the juices drop onto the surface of the dough. Scatter the olives over the surface as well. Push down gently on the olives and the tomatoes to embed them in the dough. Scatter on the oregano.

COVER loosely and set aside to rise until puffy and bubbly, about 45 minutes.

WHEN the dough is almost fully risen, preheat the oven to 475°F.

BAKE until the water has evaporated and the surface is nicely browned, 20 to 30 minutes.

PANZEROTTI
FRIED TURNOVERS

Makes 8 turnovers

Panzerotti are small turnovers from Puglia that are filled and fried. The classic filling is basil and mozzarella, but, as with pizza toppings, you can let your imagination run wild. Just be sure to seal the turnovers firmly so nothing leaks out during cooking.

2 cups bread flour

2 cups rimacinata semolina flour

1 tablespoon sugar

1 tablespoon salt

½ teaspoon instant yeast

2 tablespoons softened butter

Oil for bowl, pan, and frying

1 cup canned tomatoes, drained

1 cup drained and shredded mozzarella

8 basil leaves

IN a medium bowl combine the flours, sugar, salt, and yeast. Stir in 1 cup plus 2 tablespoons warm water and mix by hand until the dough is smooth and well combined. Add the butter and mix until incorporated.

OIL a clean bowl and transfer the dough to the oiled bowl. Cover with plastic wrap or a dishtowel and set aside to rise for 1½ hours.

DIVIDE the dough into 8 equal-sized portions. (Use a scale if you want to be exact.) Lightly oil a tray or baking sheet and set aside. Place 1 piece of dough in front of you on the work surface, smooth side up. Cup the dough with your hands and gently turn it while pressing the edges of the dough underneath so that it forms a round ball with a smooth top stretched tightly. Transfer the rounded dough to the prepared tray or pan and repeat with the remaining dough.

COVER the tray or pan with plastic wrap or a dishtowel and let rest at room temperature for 1 hour.

PLACE one ball of dough on the work surface and stretch into a thin disk, about ¼ inch thick, turning to keep the shape round as you stretch it. Set aside and repeat with remaining dough.

CRUSH the tomatoes by hand or with a fork. Place about 2 tablespoons of the tomatoes, about 2 tablespoons of the mozzarella, and one basil leaf in the center of one round of dough. Fold into a half-moon and seal the edge by pressing firmly with the heel of your hand. Repeat with remaining dough and filling.

LINE a tray or pan with paper towels. Fill a heavy pot with high sides with several inches of oil for frying. Over medium heat, bring to 375°F. Carefully slide the turnovers into the hot oil. (Work in batches if needed to keep from crowding the pot.) Fry, turning once, until golden, about 2 minutes total. Remove with the slotted spoon or skimmer and drain briefly on the prepared pan.

FARINATA

CHICKPEA FLOUR FLATBREAD

Serves 8 as an appetizer or snack

This rustic, blistered pancake showered with fresh black pepper is served up and down the coast of Liguria, as well as in the south of France. As with crepe batter, this batter needs to sit before being used. One hour is the minimum, but you can make the batter up to twelve hours in advance—the longer it sits the better. Be sure to use Italian chickpea flour and not the Indian type, which is actually made from chana dal and is toasted. Farinata is delicious paired with a crisp white wine and a few chunks of aged cheese.

1 cup chickpea flour

1 teaspoon fine sea salt

2 tablespoons extra virgin olive oil, plus more for sautéing and finishing

½ small yellow onion, thinly sliced (optional)

1 tablespoon chopped fresh rosemary (optional)

Freshly ground black pepper to taste

IN a mixing bowl, whisk together the chickpea flour and 1¾ cups water. Whisk in the salt and 2 tablespoons olive oil. Cover and set aside at room temperature for at least 1 hour and up to 12 hours.

WHEN you're ready to prepare the pancake, preheat the oven to 400°F.

IF using the onion, sauté it in olive oil over low heat until soft and translucent but not brown, about 7 minutes. Stir in the rosemary and cook for an additional 30 seconds, then remove the pan from the heat. Stir the onion into the batter.

HEAT a few teaspoons of olive oil in a 12-inch ovenproof skillet (cast iron is ideal) over medium-high heat. When the oil is hot, add the batter. Tilt the skillet if necessary to cover the surface. Bake the pancake in the oven until it is completely set and a paring knife inserted in the center comes out clean, 20 to 30 minutes. If the top has not browned, place the pancake under the broiler for 1 to 2 minutes until it is flecked with brown spots.

REMOVE the pancake from the oven and let it cool in the pan for 1 to 2 minutes. Carefully transfer the pancake to a cutting board. Cut into wedges, drizzle with your best extra virgin olive oil, and top with a very generous amount of pepper. Serve warm.

SCHIACCIATA ALL'UVA
GRAPE SCHIACCIATA

Makes one 9-inch focaccia, 6 to 8 servings

During the days of the September and October grape harvest in Toscana, dark purple canaiolo grapes are folded into lightly sweetened focaccia, locally known as *schiacciata*, or crushed. Other types of sweet focaccia in the region are made with liqueur, nuts, orange zest, and anise seed. Canaiolo grapes are sweet and small, with just the right amount of moisture, but if you can't find them near you, look for the smallest, sweetest grapes you can find. (Table grapes won't cut it.) Grape varieties are like snowflakes—no two are exactly alike. At Eataly we sell lots of interesting heirloom grapes, and smaller varieties, like tubular muscat finger grapes, would work in this recipe. Jammy Concord grapes, more readily available, will also work. Don't seed the grapes—most of the seeds will dissolve during baking, and if you cut the grapes open you'll end up with a soggy mess as they bake; when left whole they burst but don't leak.

3⅓ cups 00 flour or unbleached all-purpose flour

2¼ teaspoons instant yeast

½ cup olive oil, plus more for pan

¼ cup plus 3 tablespoons sugar

8 ounces canaiolo or other small grapes

Confectioners' sugar, for sprinkling

IN a bowl combine the flour and yeast with 1¼ cups warm water and stir to combine. Knead on a lightly floured work surface until smooth and tender, about 10 minutes. (Alternatively, knead in a stand mixer fitted with the dough hook or in a food processor fitted with the dough blade.)

LIGHTLY oil a bowl, turn the dough into the bowl, cover with plastic wrap or a dishtowel, and set aside at room temperature until doubled in size, about 2 hours.

LIGHTLY oil a 9- or 10-inch round pan with 2-inch sides.

PREHEAT the oven to 375°F.

WITH the dough still in the bowl, knead in ¼ cup sugar and ¼ cup oil. (You may find it easier to incorporate the oil while everything is still in the bowl, then transfer it to a work surface and knead there until it is fully incorporated.) It will be very sticky at first but eventually will become smooth.

PLACE the dough in the pan and gently press it with your fingertips to fill the pan. If the dough resists, set it aside to rest briefly, then try again. Pour the remaining ¼ cup of olive oil over the dough. Dimple deeply with your fingertips. Scatter the grapes over the surface. Push down gently on the grapes to embed them in the dough. Sprinkle on the remaining 3 tablespoons sugar.

BAKE in the preheated oven until the dough is golden and the grapes are soft and collapsed, about 55 minutes. Let the focaccia cool in the pan on a rack for 10 minutes. Place a cutting board or plate over the top of the pan. Invert the focaccia and lift off the pan. Turn the focaccia right side up. Replace any grapes that have come off and allow the focaccia to cool to room temperature before sprinkling with confectioners' sugar.

FOCACCIA DOLCE
SWEET FOCACCIA

Makes one 12 by 17-inch focaccia, 8 to 10 servings

This not-too-sweet focaccia, similar to a brioche bread topped with fruit and/or chocolate, is perfect for a snack. It can be enjoyed as is or split in half lengthwise and filled with chocolate spread or jam. We also like it for breakfast. You can leave off the toppings if you prefer a plain version. This is a slippery dough that requires lengthy kneading, but if you persist, you'll find that it transforms into a smooth, tender ball. Refrigerate it for a slow rise that develops flavor and also makes it much easier to handle.

1 stick plus 6 tablespoons unsalted butter

2 ounces (about ¼ cup) lievito madre (page 16)

3⅓ cups 00 flour or unbleached all-purpose flour

¼ cup sugar

1½ teaspoons fine sea salt

1½ teaspoons instant yeast

2 large eggs, lightly beaten

Olive oil for bowl

½ cup chopped chocolate, raspberries, blueberries, blackberries, sliced strawberries, or a combination for topping

CUT all but 1 tablespoon of the butter into cubes and set aside to soften.

IN a small bowl, break up the lievito madre in ⅓ cup water. In a large bowl, combine the flour, 3 tablespoons sugar, salt, and yeast. In a small bowl, break up the lievito madre in ⅓ cup water. Make a well in the center and add the eggs and the lievito madre, then gradually incorporate the liquid into the dry ingredients.

TURN the mixture onto an unfloured work surface and, using a bench scraper, knead it until it is smooth and well-combined and you can easily form a gluten window with the dough (page 88), about 15 minutes. Return the dough to the bowl and add an additional ⅓ cup water about 2 teaspoons at a time, kneading in the bowl between additions. When the water has all been incorporated, return the dough (which will be very wet) to the unfloured work surface and press it gently into a square. Scatter about one third of the softened butter over the top of the dough and knead until the butter is incorporated. Again, the dough will be very wet, so use the bench scraper. Continue to add the remaining softened butter, a few cubes at a time, kneading to combine between additions. Once the butter has been incorporated, knead the dough until it is smooth and uniform and lifts cleanly off the work surface, about 10 minutes. At first, you will not be able to knead the dough as you

would a typical bread dough—the process is more like pulling taffy. Gradually, as you knead it, it will smooth out and become more cooperative. (Alternatively, knead the dough in a food processor fitted with the dough blade or a stand mixer fitted with the dough hook.)

TRANSFER the dough to a lightly oiled bowl. Cover tightly and let rise in the refrigerator for 8 to 12 hours. The dough will increase in volume but may not fully double. Use a glass bowl if you have one—looking at the bottom will allow you to see if the dough is aerated.

OIL the bottom and sides of a half-sheet pan. Transfer the dough to the pan and press it into the pan as evenly as you can. (The dough will feel like wet clay, and the surface may be dry, even though you covered the bowl tightly.) Cover loosely with a dishtowel and let the dough sit at room temperature for 2 hours.

PREHEAT the oven to 500°F. Spread the toppings on top of the dough, dot with the remaining 1 tablespoon butter, then sprinkle on the remaining 1 tablespoon sugar. Bake in the preheated oven until the focaccia is golden and risen and the sugar on top has caramelized, 8 to 10 minutes.

PANINI

A panino is always so much more than the sum of its two parts, bread and filling.

L'ORIGINE DEL PANINO

THOUGH THE IDEA of placing a filling between two slices of bread may seem like a modern concept—a quick snack for us to grab as we dash frenetically from one place to another—the panino, or sandwich, is actually an invention dating back to ancient Rome. (Panino is also the word for a roll in Italian.)

No matter when the sandwich got its start, there's no denying that it is a genius idea: portable, tasty, a canny way of using up leftovers, and eminently satisfying. A hearty sandwich can stand as a meal on its own, but a smaller sandwich is also the perfect snack. The sandwich is also fertile ground for creativity—almost anything can be enhanced by its transformation into a filling or topping for bread.

In Italy, sandwiches are diffuse. While pizza is served in a pizzeria, and focaccia and the like are bakery products, a panino may be enjoyed at home or purchased in an *alimentari*—a small grocery store where the staff will typically allow customers to select from the cheese, cured meats, cooked vegetables, and bread and rolls behind the counter to put together their own tasty custom sandwiches. An Italian bar will usually feature sandwiches, especially tramezzini on soft sandwich bread, but also small rolls with a few slices of salami inserted between the halves. A panino makes a quick breakfast and is the perfect choice for a *schiscetta*, a lunchbox or picnic hamper—there's a reason it's the classic brown-bag lunch around the world.

PANE RUSTICO
COUNTRY-STYLE BREAD

Makes 1 medium loaf

This is Eataly's house bread, made daily using our natural yeast with a little added boost of fresh yeast. At Eataly we use a local artisanal stone-ground hard-wheat bread flour that lends an exceptionally wheaty flavor. Using a combination of lievito madre and instant yeast guarantees that this will rise reliably, yet have the slightly funky flavor the starter imparts. Because this dough is made mostly with lievito madre, it doesn't inflate drastically while proofing, but it springs into action in the oven.

4 cups bread flour

7 ounces (about 1 cup) lievito madre (page 16)

1 tablespoon fine sea salt

¼ teaspoon instant yeast

PLACE the flour in a large bowl. In a small bowl, stir the lievito madre into 1⅓ cups lukewarm water, then add this mixture to the flour and mix with a wooden spoon or by hand until the dough is shaggy. Cover the bowl tightly and set aside to rest for at least 30 minutes and up to 4 hours.

SPRINKLE on the salt and the instant yeast. Transfer the dough to an unfloured work surface. Knead until the dough is smooth and compact and forms a gluten window (page 88) about 10 minutes. The dough will start out fairly sticky and grainy feeling, but it will get smoother and easier to handle as you knead and the salt and yeast dissolve. (Alternatively, knead the dough in a food processor fitted with the dough blade or a stand mixer fitted with the dough hook.)

PLACE the dough in a proofing basket (or a colander lined with a lightly floured flat-weave dishtowel), cover loosely, and set aside to ferment at room temperature. After 30 minutes, fold and turn the dough. (To fold and turn dough, very lightly flour the dough and the work surface, then gently turn the dough onto the work surface. Pull the right side of the dough—where the 3 would be on a clock—out to the right to stretch it, then fold that stretched portion of dough over the main body of the dough. Repeat where the 6, 9, and 12 would be on a clock, pulling away and then folding the stretched portion of dough over the larger part of the dough. Turn the dough so that the smooth side is now on top and return it to the basket, using the bench scraper if needed.) After another 30 minutes, repeat this folding process. Then let the dough ferment untouched until puffy, about 1½ additional hours.

TURN the dough back onto the work surface with the smooth side down. Very gently tug the dough into a thick rectangle. (Try not to deflate the dough.) If the dough resists at any time during shaping, set it aside and come back to it 20 minutes later. Fold the dough in thirds, like a letter. Seal the seam with the flat part of your hand by rolling the dough toward you slightly and pressing the seam against the work surface. Roll the dough under the palms of your hands to round it into a tight cylinder and taper the ends.

PLACE the shaped loaf on a parchment-lined baking sheet, cover loosely, and place in the refrigerator. Proof until the dough looks very puffy and smooth and feels dry, about 8 hours. (Fermenting in the refrigerator slows the process and allows flavor to develop. If you are in a hurry, you can ferment the loaf at room temperature for a couple hours—though it will not have the same depth of flavor as bread given a longer rise.)

WHEN you are ready to bake the bread, if you are using a baking stone, place it on the middle shelf of the oven. Preheat the oven to 500°F. Place a pan on the bottom shelf of the oven for steam.

IF you have a peel and are using a baking stone, transfer the loaf (still on the parchment-lined baking sheet) to the peel. With a sharp knife or razor blade, make 1 to 4 slashes in the top of the loaf. Using the peel, slide the loaf onto the baking stone with the parchment. (If you don't have a baking stone, simply place the baking sheet in the oven.) Pour water into the pan on the bottom shelf, then quickly close the door. Bake until the bread is well-risen, the crust is dark and crisp, and you hear a hollow sound when you knock on the bottom crust, about 50 minutes.

LET the bread cool completely on a rack before slicing.

FILONCINI

LONG ROLLS

Makes six 6-inch sandwich rolls or four 8-inch sandwich rolls

---

Some sandwiches work better on individual rolls rather than sliced bread, but the process is basically the same.

4 cups bread flour

7 ounces (about 1 cup) lievito madre (page 16)

1 tablespoon fine sea salt

¼ teaspoon instant yeast

PLACE the flour in a large bowl. In a small bowl, stir the lievito madre into 1⅓ cups lukewarm water, then add this mixture to the flour and mix with a wooden spoon or by hand until the dough is shaggy. Cover the bowl tightly and set aside to rest for at least 30 minutes and up to 4 hours.

SPRINKLE on the salt and the instant yeast. Transfer the dough to an unfloured work surface. Knead until the dough is smooth and compact and forms a gluten window (page 88) about 10 minutes. The dough will start out fairly sticky and grainy feeling, but it will get smoother and easier to handle as you knead and the salt and yeast dissolve. (Alternatively, knead the dough in a food processor fitted with the dough blade or a stand mixer fitted with the dough hook.)

PLACE the dough in a proofing basket (or a colander lined with a lightly floured flat-weave dishtowel), cover loosely, and set aside to ferment at room temperature. After 30 minutes, fold and turn the dough. (To fold and turn dough, very lightly flour the dough and the work surface, then gently turn the dough onto the work surface. Pull the right side of the dough—where the 3 would be on a clock—out to the right to stretch it, then fold that stretched portion of dough over the main body of the dough. Repeat where the 6, 9, and 12 would be on a clock, pulling away and then folding the stretched portion of dough over the dough. Turn the dough so that the smooth side is now on top and return it to the basket, using the bench scraper if needed.) After another 30 minutes, repeat folding. Then let the dough ferment untouched until puffy, about 1½ additional hours.

DIVIDE the dough into 4 or 6 equal pieces. (Weigh them to be sure—judging by eye can be deceptive.) Very gently tug one piece of dough into a thick rectangle. (Try not to deflate the dough.) If the dough resists at any time during shaping, set it aside and come back to it 20 minutes later. Fold the dough in thirds, like a letter. Seal the seam with the flat part of your hand by rolling the dough toward you slightly and pressing the seam against the work surface. Roll the dough under the palms of your hands to round it into a tight cylinder and taper the ends. Repeat with remaining pieces of dough.

PLACE the shaped loaf on a parchment-lined baking sheet, cover loosely, and place in the refrigerator. Proof until the dough looks very puffy and smooth and feels dry, about 8 hours. (Fermenting in the refrigerator slows the process and allows flavor to develop. If you are in a hurry, you can ferment the loaf at room temperature for a couple hours—though it will not have the same depth of flavor as bread given a longer rise.)

WHEN you are ready to bake the rolls, preheat the oven to 450°F. Place a pan on the bottom rack of the oven for steam.

WITH a sharp knife or razor blade, slash each roll once on top. Place the baking sheet with the rolls in the oven. Pour water into the pan on the bottom shelf, then quickly close the door. Bake until the rolls are well risen, dark, and crisp, 20 to 30 minutes.

LET the rolls cool completely before slicing.

PANE

BREAD IS A GIVEN ON THE ITALIAN TABLE, where you'll never find an empty bread basket. It serves dozens of uses and can be made into breadcrumbs, used for sopping up sauce (known as *fare scarpetta,* or using the heel of the bread to clean any delicious juices remaining on your plate), and, of course, sliced for sandwiches. Depending on the size of the loaf, you may cut individual slices vertically or cut an entire loaf or roll lengthwise and fill it. Each region of Italy has its own unique breads. Below are a few of our regional favorites.

CIABATTA: Lombardia's bread with large holes in an exceptionally light crumb is known as a "slipper" due to its flat oval shape.

MAFALDA: This Sicilian semolina bread is shaped in a zigzag and topped with a scattering of sesame seeds. The same dough may also be shaped into a coiled S-shape to represent *occhi di Santa Lucia,* or Saint Lucy's eyes.

PANE DI ALTAMURA: This Puglia DOP bread is made with lievito madre and durum semolina flour that gives it a yellow tinge. Large loaves are made in various shapes, including *cappello di prete,* or priest's hat, and *accavallato,* or overlapped (known in dialect as *u sckuanète,* which rises as it bakes to resemble a pair of plump lips).

PANE DI BOLZANO: From Northern Italy comes this dense-crumbed rye bread.

PANE PUGLIESE: Puglia's loaves are large and airy. Rather than being slashed, their outsides are dimpled before they are slid into the oven to bake. The result is a dark, cracked crust and a soft interior.

PANE SCIOCCO: Toscana's bread is famously unsalted: Salt taxes were raised sky-high in the region during the twelfth century, and rather than pay up, local bakers invented saltless bread as a work-around.

PITTA: Calabria's pitta is a ring with a small hole that doesn't rise much. The dough usually incorporates lard. Often the entire loaf is sliced horizontally and filled, then cut into individual sandwiches.

ROSETTA: A rosetta is a white, airy roll imprinted with a rosette shape on top that became popular in Rome during the postwar period, when refined flour first became widely available. Milan's michetta and Bergamo's stellina are similar. See page 133 to make your own.

ROSETTE
ROSETTA ROLLS

Makes 6 rolls

Rome's rosette (the singular is rosetta) are sandwich rolls imprinted with a petal-and-pistils design. They are named not for the floral pattern, however, but for their fast and furious rise in the oven: these rolls are said to bloom like flowers. The resulting crumb is airy (the interior bakes up almost hollow) and the crust is lightly browned but still soft enough to be easy to chew. Professional bakers use a special machine or stamp to imprint the rolls; an apple slicer makes the perfect substitute for the home cook. Rosette are excellent all-purpose rolls, but the classic filling for a rosetta is a few slices of soft mortadella.

2²/₃ cups 00 flour or unbleached all-purpose flour, plus more for work surface and bowl

1 cup buratto flour

2½ teaspoons sugar

2 teaspoons fine sea salt

¾ teaspoon instant yeast

1 ounce (about 1 tablespoon) lievito madre (page 16)

2 tablespoons olive oil

COMBINE the flours, sugar, salt, and instant yeast in a large bowl. In a small bowl, break up the lievito madre in 1 cup warm water. Add this to the dry ingredients and stir to combine into a shaggy dough. Knead on an unfloured work surface until the mixture is smooth and well-combined and you can easily form a gluten window (page 88), about 12 minutes. Return the dough to the bowl and add an additional ¼ cup warm water a little at a time, kneading in the bowl to combine between additions. Transfer the dough to the unfloured work surface and knead, using a bench scraper, until it is smooth and no longer sticky, about 8 minutes. (Alternatively, knead the dough in a food processor fitted with the dough blade or a stand mixer fitted with the dough hook.) Transfer the dough to a lightly floured bowl, cover tightly, and allow to rise at room temperature until doubled, about 2 hours.

TRANSFER the dough to a lightly floured work surface and divide it into 6 equal-sized pieces, preferably using a scale to weigh them. Place one piece of dough on a lightly floured work surface, gently flatten, then roll the dough up tightly into a rough cylinder. Place it seam-side up, turn it 90 degrees (so the seam is perpendicular to you), and roll it up again. Now flip the piece of dough seam side down, cup your hands around it, and rotate it to form a sphere. The bottom of the dough should stick slightly to the board as you do this, and a taut skin should form on top. When the roll is formed, set it aside and repeat with the remaining pieces of dough.

PLACE the rolls on a parchment-lined baking sheet, cover, and let them sit at room temperature for 30 minutes. After 30 minutes, brush the tops of the rolls with olive oil and stamp each one with a rosetta stamp or apple slicer, pressing it firmly but not all the way through. Turn the rolls over, cut sides down, cover, and let them rest at room temperature for another 1½ hours.

PREHEAT the oven to 500°F. Turn the rolls cut sides up and bake until they are golden and risen, about 15 minutes.

ALLOW to cool completely before serving.

L'ACQUA

WATER IS THE STEALTH INGREDIENT IN MUCH ITALIAN COOKING. It is used to boil, braise, and steam all sorts of foods. Water is even said to make the difference in Italian coffee. When it comes to baking bread, water is crucial.

Yeast is a living thing that performs differently depending on temperature. (See page 14 for more on yeast.) Because of this, you can't simply toss ice-cold or boiling water into a bread dough and expect it to perform. The water you add to yeast doughs (including those made with lievito madre) should be warm but not hot—about the temperature of a warm bath. If the water is cooler, your dough may take longer to rise. You should never use water so hot that you cannot comfortably dip your finger into it. If you are using a food processor or a stand mixer to knead the dough, you may want to start out with slightly cooler water, as those appliances tend to heat up the dough with their rapid movement.

Italians believe firmly in the concept of *terroir*, not just for wine, but for water. Serious bakers attempting to recreate regional breads will even incorporate bottled water from the place where the loaves they are producing originated. Tap water does vary in flavor from place to place, and if your local tap water is excessively hard (high in mineral content), chlorinated (sometimes used in extremely low doses to remove dangerous organisms), or sulfurous, it may inhibit rising, especially when it comes to breads made with lievito madre. If you suspect your water is keeping your dough from blossoming the way it should, try making a loaf with filtered or bottled water. You may find the difference makes the extra effort worthwhile.

All the recipes in this book prescribe adding specific amounts of water to the dough, but that number is always flexible. There are so many factors involved in bread dough that no one precise measurement will work perfectly every time in every kitchen. Always use your judgement when adding water. Is there flour in the bottom of the bowl that refuses to be incorporated, no matter how long you knead? Add about 2 teaspoons of water at a time until you have a soft, smooth dough. Conversely, does the recipe say that the dough should be firm but you find it rather gloppy and sticky? Add about 1 teaspoon of flour at a time until you achieve the desired result. Trust your instincts and your hands and eyes and you will never go wrong.

PANINI SOFFICI
SOFT SANDWICH ROLLS

Makes 4 large or 6 small round or long rolls

Sometimes you want a soft, tender roll rather than a crusty one. These fit the bill, and they can be either round or long.

2⅔ cups 00 flour or unbleached all-purpose flour, plus more for work surface and bowl

1 cup buratto flour

2½ teaspoons sugar

2 teaspoons fine sea salt

¾ teaspoon instant yeast

1 ounce (about 1 tablespoon) lievito madre (page 16)

2 tablespoons whole milk

COMBINE the flours, sugar, salt, and instant yeast in a large bowl. In a small bowl, break up the lievito madre in 1 cup warm water and stir to combine into a shaggy dough. Knead on an unfloured work surface until the mixture is smooth and well-combined and you can easily form a gluten window (page 90), about 12 minutes. Return the dough to the bowl and add an additional ¼ cup warm water a little at a time, kneading in the bowl to combine between additions. Transfer the dough to the unfloured work surface and knead, using a bench scraper, until it is smooth and no longer sticky, about 8 minutes. (Alternatively, knead the dough in a food processor fitted with the dough blade or a stand mixer fitted with the dough hook.) Transfer the dough to a lightly floured bowl, cover tightly, and allow to rise at room temperature until doubled, about 2 hours.

TRANSFER the dough to a lightly floured work surface and divide it into 6 equal-sized pieces, preferably using a scale to weigh them. Place one piece of dough on a lightly floured work surface, gently flatten, then roll the dough up tightly into a rough cylinder. Place it seam-side up, turn it 90 degrees (so the seam is perpendicular to you), and roll it up again. Now flip the piece of dough seam side down, cup your hands around it, and rotate it to form a sphere. The bottom of the dough should stick slightly to the board as you do this, and a taut skin should form on top. When the roll is formed, set it aside and repeat with the remaining pieces of dough. For long rolls, very gently tug one piece of dough into a thick rectangle. (Try not to deflate the dough.) If at any time during shaping the dough resists, set it aside and come back to it 20 minutes later. Fold the dough in thirds like a letter. Seal the seam with the flat part of your hand by rolling the dough toward you slightly and pressing the seam together against the work surface. Roll the dough under the palms of your hands to round it into a tight cylinder and taper the ends. Repeat with remaining pieces of dough.

PLACE the rolls on a parchment-lined baking sheet, cover, and let them proof at room temperature until puffy, about 2 hours.

PREHEAT the oven to 500°F. Brush the tops of the rolls with the milk. With a sharp knife or razor blade, slash each roll once on top. Place the baking sheet with the rolls in the oven. Bake until the rolls are well risen and golden, about 20 minutes.

SALUMI

A panino with prosciutto, or *panis ac perna,* was the original Italian street food sandwich, and it remains a favorite today. After all, who could resist prosciutto crudo, salted pork thigh that slices into silky and salty-sweet dark pink sheets with a ring of white fat around the perimeter? At Eataly we offer five different types of DOP prosciutto, each one the perfect filling for a sandwich:

PROSCIUTTO DI PARMA: Probably the most famous type of prosciutto crudo. Prosciutto has been made in the Parma area for as far back as 100 B.C.E. It is sweet and delicate.

PROSCIUTTO DI TOSCANO: Toscana's reigning prosciutto is salted and spiced with juniper, rosemary, and black pepper.

PROSCIUTTO DI MODENA: Prosciutto from Modena, in northern Emilia-Romagna, is a little less salty than other types. It pairs particularly well with cheese.

PROSCIUTTO DI CARPEGNA: Prosciutto di Carpegna, from the Marche, dates back to the Middle Ages, when salt-curing as a method of preserving meat was gaining popularity. This type of prosciutto is made from the pesante Padano breed of pigs.

PROSCIUTTO DI SAN DANIELE: From Friuli Venezia Giulia, this prosciutto is pressed, which allows the salt to penetrate the meat more deeply and gives the hock a distinctive guitar shape.

There are many other cured meats that make for excellent panini. In their simplest form, you can drape thin slices of salami inside a roll and call it a day, but the options for embellishments are endless. Keep an eye on how salty each ingredient is to maintain balance.

BRESAOLA: Dark red beef that is first salted and then air-dried.

COPPA: Known in some areas as capocolla, this salami is made from a pig's neck; the tongue and ear cartilage form a white web visible when the salami is sliced. The coppa of Piacenza is a DOP product. It is also made in Calabria, Umbria, and the Marche.

CULATELLO DI ZIBELLO: According to DOP standards, culatello is made from a large muscle mass from a pig's back leg stuffed into a pig's bladder and slowly aged in special cellars.It is available only a few months out of the year and only in select places. We're extremely proud to offer it at Eataly.

FINOCCHIONA: Pork belly and shoulder salami with fennel seeds from Toscana.

LARDO: Pork fat flavored with pepper, garlic, and herbs, then salted and aged.

PROSCIUTTO COTTO: Cooked ham with a delicate flavor and moist texture.

MORTADELLA: Bologna's rosy pink specialty, made from minced lean pork with cubes of fat (and sometimes pistachios).

SALAME FELINO: Pork salami from the village of Felino in central Emilia-Romagna, which sits 607 feet above sea level and has the perfect microclimate for curing. Seasoned with black peppercorns, white wine, and garlic.

SALAME MILANO: Fine-grained brick-red pork and beef salami.

SOPPRESSATA: Also known as testa in cassetta, soppressata is a dried pork salami that includes parts of the head, roughly chopped so that slices of the finished salami resemble a mosaic.

SPECK: Lean pork leg from Trentino–Alto Adige that's salted and seasoned with juniper, bay leaves, and rosemary, then dry-cured, smoked, and briefly aged.

PANINI REGIONALI TIPICI

NOT ONLY DOES EACH REGION OF ITALY HAVE ITS OWN BREAD, its own cured meats, and its own cheeses but most regions have their own particular sandwiches. These are often the ultimate in Italy's *cucina povera,* the nation's waste-not-want-not culinary repertoire. Many of the best examples are sold out of trucks or at market stalls.

In Firenze, a lampredotto is a crusty bun slathered with a piquant green sauce of parsley, garlic, and anchovies, and then filled with cow innards—a specific chamber of the bovine stomach—boiled with herbs until tender. The name comes from lamprey, or eel, a delicacy enjoyed by the aristocracy; those without the means to enjoy eel deemed this sandwich their own version.

In nearby Arezzo, a **PAN CO' GRIFI** is made with the muscles from a calf's snout stewed in red wine and spiced with cloves.

A **PANINO CON LE SPUNTATURE** from the Marche region is filled with hot grilled calf's intestines sprinkled with copious amounts of black pepper.

MORZELLO (or *morzeddu*) from Catanzaro is a mix of various cow organ meats cooked with tomatoes and hot peppers for 5 or 6 hours, then stuffed into a curved slice of pitta, Calabria's ring-shaped bread.

PANE CON LA MILZA, *pani cà meusa* in local dialect, is a Palermitano treat of a roll filled with cow's spleen and lungs, and traditionally a little of the windpipe as well. This may be topped off with ricotta, caciocavallo, or a squirt of lemon juice.

If organ meats aren't your thing, Palermo also has a vegetarian specialty, **PANE E PANELLE,** consisting of chickpea flour fritters served on a sesame seed roll. The rectangular fritters are made by cooking a sort of porridge of chickpea flour and water, spreading it into a sheet, and allowing it to cool, then cutting it into fingers and frying them until crisp.

FOCACCIA FARCITA

PLAIN FOCACCIA CAN BE SLICED HORIZONTALLY AND FILLED, then cut into squares or rectangles. We particularly like to serve these tasty sandwiches at a picnic. Use the Focaccia per Panini on page 91. You can make the focaccia up to 24 hours in advance and leave it at room temperature, but fill the sandwiches an hour or so before you want to eat. You can also bake a round Focaccia Barese (page 109) without any toppings except for the salamoia and then slice lengthwise, fill, and cut into wedges. Whatever you choose, never slice bread until it has cooled completely: rather than having a clean cut, it will get mashed. Always drizzle a little olive oil on the filling before closing the sandwiches.

BOSCAIOLO: Sautéed mixed mushrooms, taleggio, arugula

CALABRESE: Spicy soppressata, sliced provolone

UMBRO: Sliced roasted pork loin, shaved fennel, capers

ALPINO: Prosciutto cotto, sliced fontina, fig mostarda

SICILIANO: Ricotta, roasted zucchini, marinated artichokes, caponata

MARINAIO: Olive-oil poached tuna, sliced tomatoes, arugula, olive paste

CONTADINO: Soft-boiled egg, capers, sliced tomatoes

BOLOGNESE: Mortadella, Parmigiano Reggiano shavings, arugula

PANINO CAPRESE

MOZZARELLA AND TOMATO SANDWICH

Makes 4 sandwiches

The idyllic island of Capri, off the coast of Napoli, is known for its winding, bougainvillea-lined streets and staggeringly beautiful views—and for the genius combination of mozzarella, fresh tomatoes, and basil, which may be featured in a salad or used as a filling for a sandwich. This is one of our most popular sandwiches at Eataly and a classic all over Italy. Because it is simple, using the best ingredients is key. Only in-season juicy tomatoes and tender high-quality mozzarella (we make this with our housemade mozzarella) will do.

4 squares Focaccia per Panini (page 91)

8 ounces mozzarella

2 large beefsteak tomatoes

Leaves of 2 sprigs basil

2 tablespoons extra virgin olive oil

WITH a serrated knife, split the squares of focaccia lengthwise. Place the bottom of each square on a plate. Slice the mozzarella into 8 to 10 slices, about ½ inch thick. Divide the slices among the 4 rolls, arranging them overlapping slightly if necessary to fit in a single layer. Slice the tomatoes into ½-inch slices and arrange them on top of the mozzarella, again overlapping slightly if necessary to fit but maintaining a single layer. Place a few leaves of basil on top of each, then drizzle the olive oil on top. Top each sandwich with the top half of the focaccia square.

SERVE at room temperature and never refrigerate.

FORMAGGI

One of the best and simplest sandwiches you can make consists of delicious cheese between two slices of bread or a square of focaccia.

ASIAGO: Asiago from the Veneto region is a pale yellow DOP cheese that may be brined and aged for about one month for Asiago pressato or aged for up to fifteen months for a sharper taste and firmer texture.

BURRATA: From the Murge area of Puglia, burrata takes the form of a solid pouch of mozzarella with a liquid center made up of cream and stracciatella, "little rags" or shreds of mozzarella left over from cheesemaking. It is best left whole so that the diner can cut it and allow the creamy interior to escape. It is always served at room temperature.

CACIOCAVALLO: This is a drawn curd cheese from the southern Apennines. It is formed into water balloon shapes and tied together in pairs with rope to be hung for aging (or to be transported on the back of a donkey or horse, as the name indicates). This pairs well with spicy and salty partners, such as olive spread or pickled hot peppers.

FONTINA: A semi-firm creamy cow's milk cheese with a funky hint of mushroom flavor, fontina melts beautifully.

MOZZARELLA: Our housemade mozzarella can be sliced and included in sandwiches like a classic Panino Caprese (page 145).

PARMIGIANO REGGIANO: Parmigiano isn't a slicing cheese, but you can cut shavings of it with a vegetable peeler or paring knife and use them to add a savory taste to almost any sandwich. Parmigiano shavings pair particularly well with peppery arugula.

PECORINO: Pecorino is a catch-all word for sheep's milk cheese and may be soft and fresh or aged until quite firm.

PIAVE: Straw-colored Piave may be either vecchio (aged) or stravecchio (extra-aged), developing a more intense flavor and grainy texture as it ages.

PROVOLONE: Provolone is a semihard and very smooth cheese whose taste can range from mild to spicy. It melts very well.

RICOTTA: Ricotta is actually not a cheese but a cheesemaking byproduct. Spreadable and mild, it makes an excellent base for crostini.

ROBIOLA: Soft cheese made with cow's, goat's, or sheep's milk—or a combination—this Piemonte native is tangy and spreadable.

STRACCHINO: Acidic and spreadable stracchino marries well with peppery fresh arugula.

PANE IN CASSETTA

SANDWICH BREAD

Makes one 13 x 4-inch loaf

Caffè Mulassano in Torino lays claim to inventing tramezzini—the Italian answer to tea sandwiches—in 1926, and it was famed Italian writer Gabriele D'Annunzio who invented the word. Today you will find tramezzini in bars all over Italy, inevitably displayed the same way it was about one hundred years ago: the crustless sandwiches are cut on the diagonal into triangles and stacked on trays, then covered with a damp towel to keep the surfaces from drying out. At Eataly we make dozens of tramezzini every morning. The variety of the fillings is endless, but only one type of bread is used: this soft white sandwich bread, known in Italy as pancarré (French for square bread) or pane in cassetta, meaning bread in a box. Both names reference the fact that this bread is baked in a Pullman loaf pan, which has a sliding lid that keeps it perfectly square in shape. If you don't have a Pullman loaf pan, place about three quarters of this dough in a standard loaf pan and shape the remainder into rolls, then trim off the rounded top of each slice when you're trimming the crusts to make the sandwiches.

4¾ cups 00 flour or unbleached all-purpose flour

1 tablespoon instant yeast

1 large egg, lightly beaten

¼ cup whole milk, room temperature

2 tablespoons sugar

1 tablespoon fine sea salt

6 tablespoons unsalted butter, cut into cubes and softened, plus more for pan

COMBINE the flour, yeast, egg, milk, and 1 teaspoon sugar in a large bowl and stir in ¾ cup warm water. Stir to combine into a shaggy dough. Knead on an unfloured work surface until the mixture is smooth and well-combined, about 5 minutes. Flatten the dough slightly on the work surface and sprinkle on the salt and remaining sugar. Knead until the salt and sugar are evenly distributed. Gently flatten the dough into a rectangle and add 2 tablespoons of the butter. Knead, using a bench scraper, until the butter is incorporated. Add the remaining butter in 2 to 3 more additions, kneading to combine between additions. Knead until the dough is soft and well-combined and cleans the work surface. (Alternatively, knead the dough in a food processor fitted with the dough blade or a stand mixer fitted with the dough hook.)

TRANSFER the dough to a bowl, cover, and let rise at room temperature until doubled in size, 1½ to 2 hours.

GENEROUSLY butter a 13 x 4-inch Pullman pan. Transfer the dough to a lightly floured work surface and very lightly flour the top. Flip the dough over. Gently shape the dough into a rectangle. Fold the bottom up to the middle, then fold in the right and left sides. Roll the dough down from the top toward you, shaping it into a fat log. Turn the dough over into the prepared pan so that it is seam-side down. Cover and let rise until it reaches just below the top of the pan, 1½ to 2½ hours.

PREHEAT the oven to 350°F. Place the lid on the pan and bake until golden, about 50 minutes.

TURN the bread out of the pan and allow it to cool completely on a rack before slicing.

TRAMEZZINI

TRAMEZZINI ARE THE VERY OPPOSITE of a busting-at-the-seams overstuffed sandwich. They were initially invented as a snack to tide one over between meals and are often enjoyed with a glass of wine as an appetizer. The filling should be the same thickness as one slice of bread, about ¼ inch.

1. Stack 2 slices of Pane in Cassetta (page 147) on a work surface. Trim off the crusts. (Save the crusts and the heels of the bread for breadcrumbs.)

2. Set the 2 slices of bread side by side. Thinly spread the bread with a very small amount of spread, which may be softened butter, mayonnaise, or mustard. Arrange or spread the filling (see below for suggestions) evenly over the surface of one slice in a thin layer, making sure to spread it all the way out to the edges.

3. Place the other piece of bread on top of the filling. With a sharp knife, cut on a diagonal into 2 triangles.

4. Arrange the filled tramezzini on a tray or plate. Wet a dishtowel under running water, then wring it out thoroughly. Drape the dishtowel over the sandwiches and refrigerate. Bring to room temperature at least 30 minutes before serving.

FILLINGS

Mustard, prosciutto cotto, Asiago, Little Gem lettuce

Cultured butter, sliced hard-boiled eggs, caviar, endive

Mayonnaise, drained canned tuna combined with diced red bell pepper, diced celery, diced red onion, minced parsley, and mayonnaise,
thin slices of tart green apple

Butter, bresaola, sliced mozzarella, baby arugula

Mayonnaise, crabmeat folded with mayonnaise and a pinch of ground chili pepper

Mayonnaise, chopped cooked lobster folded with mayonnaise, shavings of black truffle

Butter, minced mortadella and pistachios folded with whipped ricotta

PANINO DI MANZO

PRIME RIB SANDWICH

Makes 6 sandwiches

This hearty sandwich has become a signature at Eataly stores in the United States, where it is served juicy and warm in the La Rosticceria section of our markets. We use Black Angus beef from Creekstone Farms in Kansas. Seek out similarly high-quality prime rib. This is a snap to assemble at the last minute, and the beef actually improves if it has time to sit for a while after roasting. We like to make these on our Filoncini rolls (page 128) but they also work on focaccia or any other type of bread.

1 ounce dried porcini mushrooms

1 tablespoon fine sea salt

¼ cup light brown sugar

1 tablespoon freshly ground black pepper

1½ teaspoons crushed red pepper

1 4-pound boneless prime rib

6 Filoncini (page 128) or other rolls

Olive oil for drizzling

Flaky sea salt to taste

IN a blender, process the dried porcini to a very fine powder. Combine the porcini powder, fine sea salt, brown sugar, black pepper, and red pepper in a bowl. Rub the prime rib all over with the porcini mixture. Cover tightly and refrigerate for 24 hours.

PREHEAT the oven to 450°F. Transfer the prime rib to a roasting pan and roast until it reaches an internal temperature in the center of 130°F, 30 to 45 minutes. Allow the meat to rest for 15 minutes before slicing.

TO assemble the sandwiches, slice each roll in half lengthwise. Slice the meat thinly, but not paper-thin, and arrange a generous amount of meat on the bottom of each roll. Drizzle each serving with olive oil, season with flaky salt, and top with the other half of each roll.

PANINO DI PORCHETTA
PORCHETTA SANDWICH

Makes 6 sandwiches

Porchetta hails from central Italy, where at outdoor events carts often sell succulent sandwiches made of thick slices of porchetta on rolls. Be sure to drizzle each sandwich with some of the juices from the porchetta.

¼ cup sugar

1½ cups fine sea salt, plus more for seasoning belly

4 pounds boneless pork loin, sinew and fat trimmed

¾ cup fennel seeds

¾ cup black peppercorns

4 pounds boneless pork belly with skin

2 tablespoons minced garlic

6 Panini Soffici (page 138)

Extra virgin olive oil for drizzling

PLACE the sugar and ½ cup salt in a container that is large enough to hold the pork loin in the brine. Bring a large pot of water (about 1 gallon) to a boil and pour into the container. Whisk until the salt and sugar are dissolved. Add a generous amount of ice to cool the water—you want enough liquid to fully submerge the loin. Place the loin in the cold brine (add water to cover if needed) and refrigerate for 24 hours.

IN a spice grinder, grind the fennel seeds and black peppercorns. Combine with the remaining 1 cup salt. Reserve about half of this spice mixture in a small bowl and set aside.

SEASON the pork belly with the other half of the spice mixture; discard any that isn't used. Cover the pork belly and refrigerate for at least 8 hours.

WHEN you are ready to roast the porchetta, preheat the oven to 350°F. Combine the reserved spice mixture with the minced garlic and stir to combine.

REMOVE the loin from the brine and pat dry. (Discard the brine.) Completely coat the loin and the pork belly with the garlic spice mixture. Use some of the reserved rub, if needed, to cover all of the meat's surface area. Wrap the belly around the pork loin so that the loin is completely covered. Truss the meat with twine, tying knots about 1 inch apart. (The easiest way to do this is to start in the middle of the porchetta and work your way to the ends.) Place the porchetta on a rack set in a roasting pan. Place in the preheated oven and cook until the middle of the pork loin reaches an internal temperature of 138°F and the skin is crispy, which will likely take at least 1 hour 15 minutes but may take up to 2 hours. Allow the porchetta to rest 10 minutes before slicing.

CUT the rolls in half lengthwise. Slice the porchetta into ½- to ¾-inch-thick slices. Arrange several slices on the bottom of each roll. Drizzle with some of the juices and a little olive oil. Top with the top halves of the rolls and serve.

PANINI GRIGLIATI

SOMETHING FUNNY HAPPENED as the word *panino* travelled from Italy to the United States. While to Italians the word simply means a sandwich of any type (or a roll), on the other side of the Atlantic it has come to mean a warm sandwich toasted in a sandwich press. In Italy we refer to these as panini grigliati, or pressed sandwiches (or, in case the linguistic back-and-forth wasn't confusing enough for you, if a warm sandwich is made on toasted sandwich bread it will often be labeled "un toast" in Italian). No matter what you call it, a warm sandwich is always delicious, especially if it contains cheese that melts appealingly in the heat.

If you have a sandwich press, obviously, that will make excellent sandwiches. If you don't have a sandwich press, use a cast-iron pan or a griddle and press down on the sandwich with a lid that is slightly smaller in diameter than the pan so that you can press the outer surface of the sandwich against the hot surface of the pan, turning once about halfway through.

For each sandwich you'll need 1 horizontally sliced square of Pizza alla Pala Bianca (page 186) or any sturdy bread or roll of your choice. Fill it with the ingredients, place the filling inside, assemble, and cook until any cheese has melted and the outside of the sandwich is golden and toasty, 4 to 5 minutes total.

HERE ARE SOME OF OUR FAVORITE COMBINATIONS AT EATALY:

Mushrooms sautéed with garlic, parsley and fontina

Spicy soppressata, provolone, and drained giardiniera (pickled vegetables)

Prosciutto cotto and fontina

Sautéed greens, caramelized onions, and Asiago

Speck, crucolo, radicchio, and a drizzle of balsamic vinegar

Sausage and sautéed bell peppers

CROSTINI E BRUSCHETTE

THE OPEN-FACED SANDWICHES known as crostini and bruschette make versatile and simple appetizers or snacks. Crostini are made with bread sliced about ¾ inch thick and toasted until crisp. For bruschette, the bread is sliced at least 1 inch thick and often grilled and rubbed with a garlic clove for extra flavor. Slices of Pane Rustico (page 125) are perfect for this purpose. You will need about 1 tablespoon of topping per slice, and the possibilities are almost endless.

CROSTINI CON CANNELLINI: By hand, roughly mash cooked white beans with plenty of freshly ground black pepper. Spread on toast and garnish with minced pickled red onion and parsley.

CROSTINI CON TONNO: Drain Italian canned tuna and puree with capers until smooth. Spread on toast and garnish with whole capers.

CROSTINI CON ZUCCA: Roast winter squash until tender, then puree with salt; garnish with shavings of aged pecorino.

CROSTINI CON PISELLI: This makes a nice spring treat. Blanch fresh shelled peas, drain, and combine with finely grated lemon zest, oil, and salt. Spread ricotta on bread, then top with the peas. Garnish with torn fresh mint leaves.

CROSTINI CON ASIAGO, SPECK, E MIELE: Toast the bread, and while it is still warm sprinkle with grated Asiago cheese. (If the bread has cooled so much that the cheese doesn't melt, pop it back into the oven or toaster oven for a few minutes.) Top each with a thin slice of speck and a drizzle of honey.

CROSTINI TOSCANI: Spread chicken liver pâté on toasted bread.

BRUSCHETTE ALL'AGLIO: The original garlic bread, also known as fettunta, or oiled bread. Rub the surface of the toasted or grilled bread with a cut garlic clove. Drizzle with copious amounts of olive oil and season with salt.

BRUSCHETTE AL POMODORO: Chop ripe summer tomatoes and toss with salt and olive oil. Toast the bread, rub the surface with a garlic clove, then spoon the tomatoes and their juices over the top.

BRUSCHETTE SICILIANE: Rub the surface of the bread with a cut garlic clove. Brush with oil. Combine ricotta with minced fresh oregano, crushed red pepper flakes, and minced black olives. Spread the mixture on the bread.

PIADINA CON FORMAGGIO FRESCO E RUCOLA

PIADINA WITH FRESH CHEESE AND ARUGULA

Makes 6 filled flatbreads

Rustic piadine flatbreads are one of the signature dishes of the Romagna area, where they are folded around simple fillings into half-moons. Creamy fresh cheese is a classic pairing with piadine, but they are also great with prosciutto and other cured meats, or sautéed greens. A piadina is not crisp like a cracker or soft like a crepe but somewhere in between. If you are lard-averse (and if you are we encourage you to rethink your prejudice—lard is delicious and not unhealthy in small amounts) you can make these with olive oil. They will be very tasty when freshly made, but any leftovers will turn crisp and cracker-like rather than remaining pliable.

2 cups 00 flour or unbleached all-purpose flour

2 teaspoons fine sea salt

½ teaspoon baking soda

¼ cup whole milk

¼ cup melted leaf lard or extra virgin olive oil

1 pound fresh cheese, such as stracchino, crescenza, or squacquerello

3 cups tightly packed baby arugula

PLACE the flour, salt, and baking soda in a bowl and combine.

IN a measuring cup with a spout, whisk together the milk and lard. Add the liquid to the dry ingredients in a thin stream, mixing with a fork as you do.

FILL the measuring cup with ½ cup room temperature water and add most but not all of it to the bowl in a thin stream, mixing constantly. You may not need all of the water (or, conversely, you may need a little more). Knead in the bowl until you have a soft, shaggy dough. Transfer the dough to a work surface and knead until very smooth and tender, about 8 minutes. You can also make the dough in a food processor fitted with the dough blade.

ON an unfloured work surface, cut the dough into 6 equal pieces, using a scale to weigh them if you want to be precise. Set aside all but one piece and cover with an overturned bowl. With a rolling pin, roll the piece of dough to a disk about 8 inches in diameter and ⅛ inch thick. Set it aside and repeat with the remaining pieces of dough. Do not stack the disks. If one piece of dough resists rolling and stretching, set it aside and go on to the next. It will relax and be easier to roll after a few minutes.

WHEN all the pieces of dough have been rolled out, heat a 10-inch cast-iron skillet or griddle over medium heat until it is hot enough that a drop of water sizzles. Place 1 disk of dough on the skillet or griddle and cook for 10 seconds. Flip and cook for an additional 10 seconds. Both sides should now look dry. Use a fork to pierce the flatbread and rotate it slightly, about one-eighth of the way around. Cook, turning occasionally with the fork, until black spots dot the underside, then flip and do the same for the other side, about 2 minutes per side. If black spots are developing too quickly or large areas are scorching, turn down the heat; if the surface of the bread remains pale and does not develop spots, turn up the heat. When the piadina is cooked, spread some of the fresh cheese on the surface and let it sit for about 10 seconds, then remove and top the cheese with some of the arugula. Fold and set aside. Repeat with the remaining disks of dough and filling, continuing to regulate the heat.

SERVE warm.

WE'VE TALKED A LOT ABOUT REGIONAL DIFFERENCES IN THIS BOOK, and the piadine on page 158 are not only made in specific regions, but vary depending on where in that region you find yourself. Along the coast of Romagna, in the area in and around Rimini, a piadina is a very thin disk; as you move further inland and up into the hills and mountains, the flatbreads grow progressively thicker. The piadina in the southern part of the region is also larger in diameter, while northern Romagna offers a smaller piadina. There are also variations without milk, and some that incorporate wine. Feel free to experiment a little and figure out your own preferences.

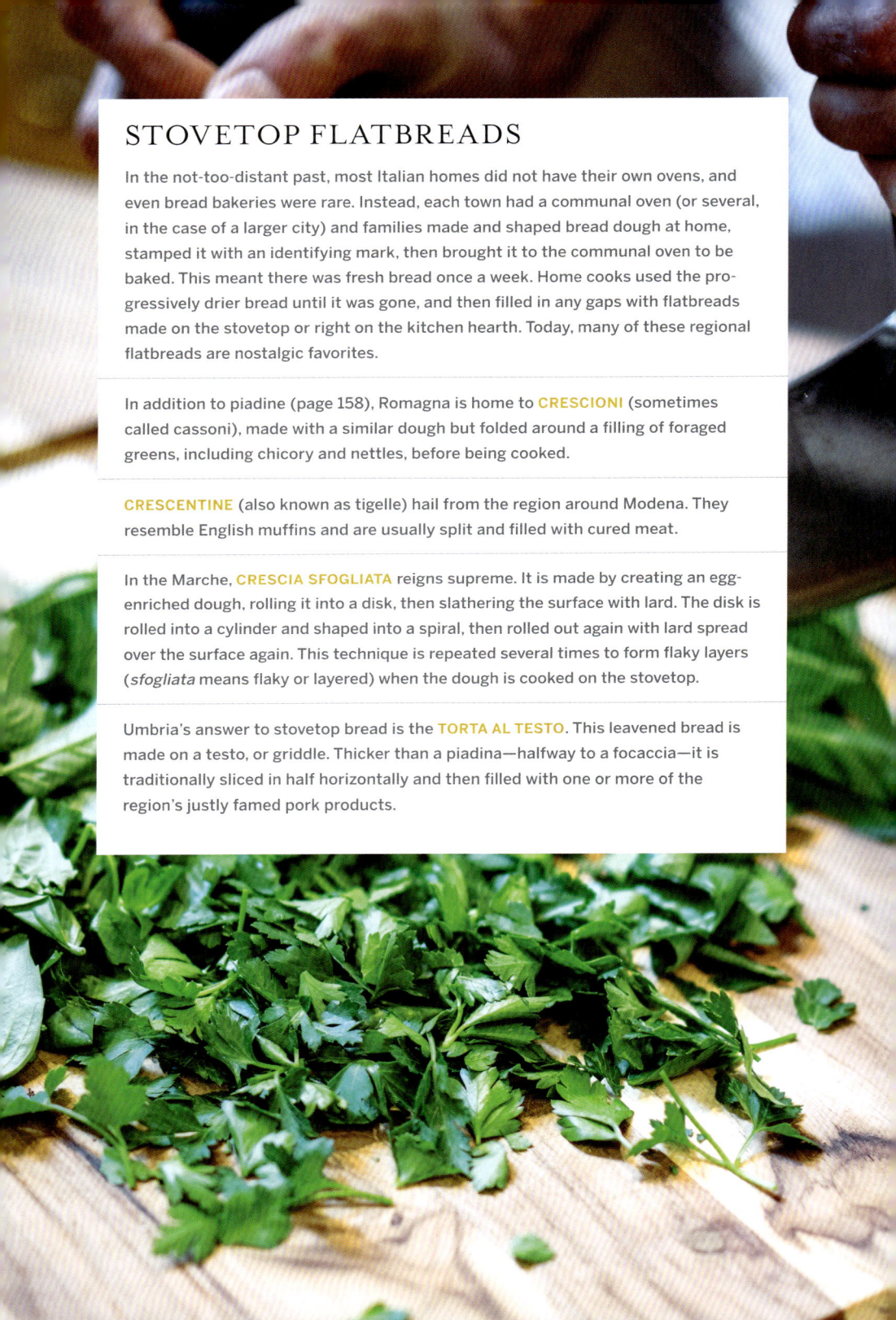

STOVETOP FLATBREADS

In the not-too-distant past, most Italian homes did not have their own ovens, and even bread bakeries were rare. Instead, each town had a communal oven (or several, in the case of a larger city) and families made and shaped bread dough at home, stamped it with an identifying mark, then brought it to the communal oven to be baked. This meant there was fresh bread once a week. Home cooks used the progressively drier bread until it was gone, and then filled in any gaps with flatbreads made on the stovetop or right on the kitchen hearth. Today, many of these regional flatbreads are nostalgic favorites.

In addition to piadine (page 158), Romagna is home to **CRESCIONI** (sometimes called cassoni), made with a similar dough but folded around a filling of foraged greens, including chicory and nettles, before being cooked.

CRESCENTINE (also known as tigelle) hail from the region around Modena. They resemble English muffins and are usually split and filled with cured meat.

In the Marche, **CRESCIA SFOGLIATA** reigns supreme. It is made by creating an egg-enriched dough, rolling it into a disk, then slathering the surface with lard. The disk is rolled into a cylinder and shaped into a spiral, then rolled out again with lard spread over the surface again. This technique is repeated several times to form flaky layers (*sfogliata* means flaky or layered) when the dough is cooked on the stovetop.

Umbria's answer to stovetop bread is the **TORTA AL TESTO**. This leavened bread is made on a testo, or griddle. Thicker than a piadina—halfway to a focaccia—it is traditionally sliced in half horizontally and then filled with one or more of the region's justly famed pork products.

CRESCENTINE MODENESI
MODENA STOVETOP FLATBREADS

Makes about 20 3-inch flatbreads

Modena's crescentine (known as tigelle in Bologna) are small disks cooked on the stovetop that resemble English muffins. They are split down the middle and filled, most often with lardo and rosemary. Traditionally, to make these, terracotta molds were buried in the embers of the kitchen fireplace until they were very hot. They were then filled with dough (and sometimes first lined with chestnut leaves) that cooked in the molds, resulting in a crisp surface and a tender center. The molds were often decorative as well, so they would imprint a design onto the surface of the flatbreads. There are also cast-iron pans with indentations made specifically for cooking crescentine. It's a lot less poetic, but you can use a cookie cutter and a griddle or cast-iron pan to achieve similar results.

4 cups 00 flour or unbleached all-purpose flour

1 teaspoon instant yeast

1 teaspoon fine sea salt

2 tablespoons lard or extra virgin olive oil, plus oil for pan

2/3 cup whole milk, room temperature

IN a large bowl combine the flour, yeast, and salt. Cut the lard into the dry ingredients or add the oil. Add the milk in a thin stream while stirring. Add lukewarm water in a thin stream until you have a tender but still shaggy dough, about 2/3 cup. Transfer the dough to a lightly floured work surface and knead until tender and smooth, about 8 minutes.

TRANSFER the dough to a clean bowl, slash an X in the top, cover with a dishtowel, and set aside to ferment at room temperature until puffy, about 1 hour.

WHEN the dough is puffy, turn it out onto a lightly floured work surface and, with a rolling pin, roll it to a little less than 1/4 inch thick. Use a 3-inch round cookie cutter to cut disks of dough. Knead any scraps together, reroll, and cut out more disks. Arrange the disks in a single layer on a work surface or a parchment-lined pan, cover with a dishtowel, and set aside at room temperature to proof until puffy, about 1 hour.

LINE a bowl or basket with a clean dishtowel. Heat a griddle or cast-iron pan over medium heat. Brush the surface very lightly with oil. Cook the flatbreads, turning once, until they are mottled and puffy, about 4 to 6 minutes total. Once they are cooked, transfer them to the towel-lined bowl or basket to keep warm until serving.

GNOCCO FRITTO

FRIED DUMPLINGS

Makes about 4 dozen dumplings

A gnocco fritto isn't quite a flatbread—it's too airy to be considered flat. These triangles of dough puff up like pillows. They're eaten steaming hot with cheese and cured meats. Like the crescentine on the previous page, they're a popular snack served with cured meats and cheeses alongside drinks.

3 cups 00 flour or unbleached all-purpose flour

1 teaspoon instant yeast

½ teaspoon fine sea salt

½ teaspoon sugar

3 tablespoons lard or extra virgin olive oil

Oil for frying

Cured meats and cheeses for serving

IN a large bowl combine the flour, yeast, salt, and sugar. Cut the lard into the dry ingredients or add the oil. Add lukewarm water in a thin stream until you have a tender but still shaggy dough, about ⅔ cup. Transfer the dough to a lightly floured work surface and knead until tender and smooth, about 8 minutes.

TRANSFER the dough to a clean bowl, slash an X in the top, cover with a dishtowel, and set aside until doubled, about 2 hours.

TURN the dough out onto a lightly floured work surface and, with a rolling pin, roll very thin, about 1/10 inch thick. Use a knife or straight pastry cutter to cut the dough into lozenges or diamonds 3 by 2¾ inches. Reroll any scraps and cut again.

LINE a sheet pan with paper towels. In a large pot or Dutch oven with high sides, heat several inches of oil for frying. Add a few of the pieces of dough (don't crowd the pan) and cook, turning once, until golden and puffed, 1 to 3 minutes total. They should remain soft without turning dark brown. Adjust heat as necessary. Once they are cooked, remove with a slotted spoon or skimmer and transfer them to the prepared pan. Repeat with remaining pieces of dough.

SERVE warm.

PANUOZZO
PIZZA SANDWICH

Makes 4 sandwiches

A panuozzo is a best-of-both-worlds combination of a pizza and a sandwich.

3 ounces Grana Padano

8 ounces cherry tomatoes

14 ounces mozzarella di bufala

1 batch Impasto per la Pizza Napoletana (page 24)

Flour for rolling

3 cups baby arugula

6 ounces thinly sliced prosciutto di Parma

Salt and freshly ground black pepper

2 tablespoons extra virgin olive oil

AT least 1 hour before you plan to bake the panuozzo, place a rack with a baking stone on the second highest shelf (with no racks above it) and preheat the oven to its highest temperature. Most home ovens go up to at least 500°F; some may go higher. It is important to preheat the oven and the stone at length. If the highest heat you can achieve in your oven is on the broil setting, preheat the oven and stone to 500°F, then switch to the broiler setting before sliding in the pizza. (Alternatively, build a fire in a wood-burning oven and bring to 850°F to 900°F.)

SHAVE the cheese with a vegetable peeler. Halve the cherry tomatoes. Slice the mozzarella. Set all three aside.

DUST the top and sides of one of the risen dough rounds generously with flour. With a floured bench scraper, scrape the dough off of the surface and flip it. Generously dust the dough round with more flour so that both sides are now floured.

GRAB the dough by opposite sides and stretch outwards into a rectangle about 8 by 4 inches. Dust an oven peel with a bit of flour and transfer the dough to the peel. Slide the dough into the oven.

THE dough should start to completely fill with air. With the peel turn the bread twice to make sure that it cooks evenly. Remove it from the oven when it is browned, puffed, and blistered, 4 to 7 minutes. (It will cook in 1 to 1½ minutes in a wood-burning oven.)

ONCE it is out of the oven slice it open lengthwise and fill it with about one-quarter each of the Grana Padano, cherry tomatoes, mozzarella, arugula, and prosciutto di Parma. Season with salt and pepper and drizzle with olive oil. Slice in half and serve warm. Repeat with remaining dough and filling.

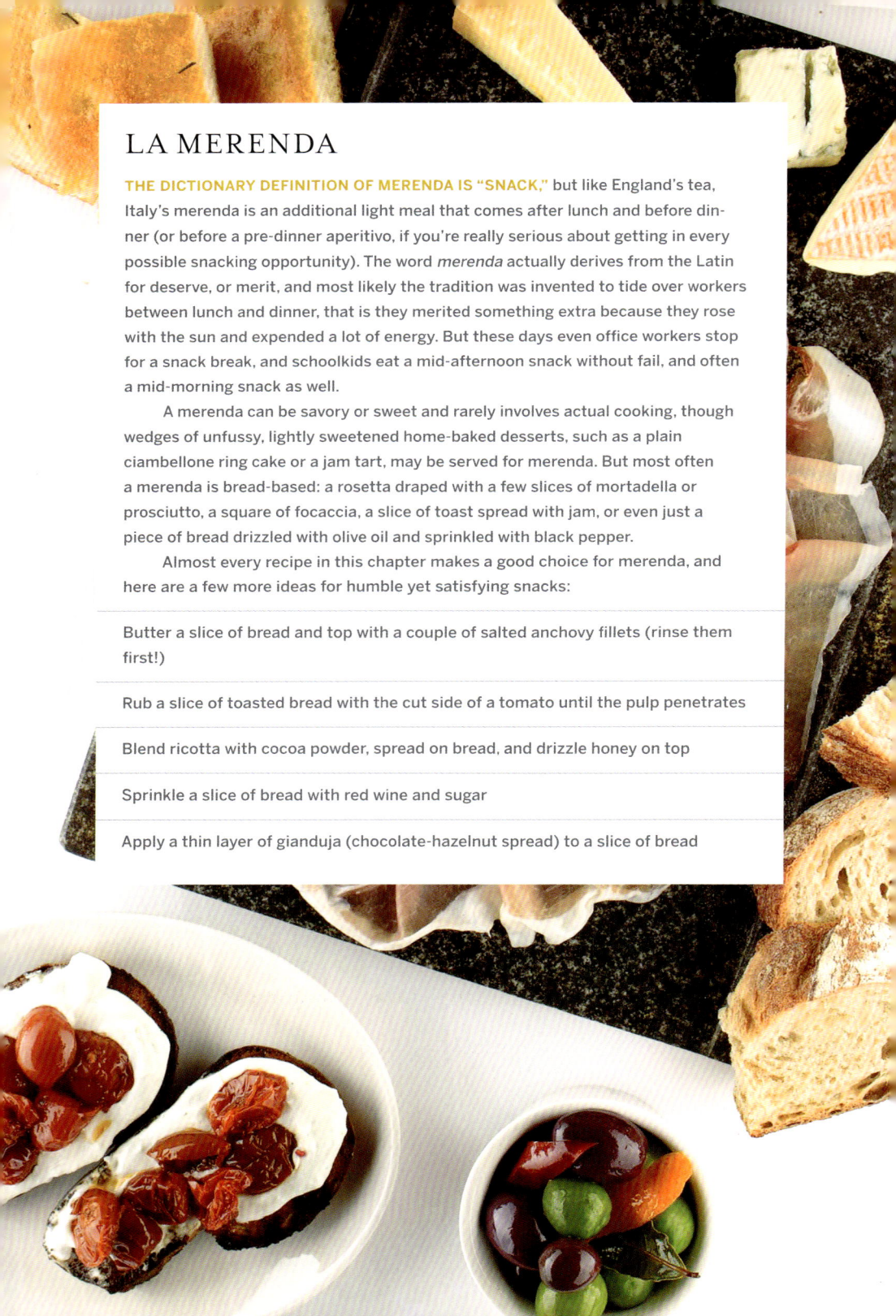

LA MERENDA

THE DICTIONARY DEFINITION OF MERENDA IS "SNACK," but like England's tea, Italy's merenda is an additional light meal that comes after lunch and before dinner (or before a pre-dinner aperitivo, if you're really serious about getting in every possible snacking opportunity). The word *merenda* actually derives from the Latin for deserve, or merit, and most likely the tradition was invented to tide over workers between lunch and dinner, that is they merited something extra because they rose with the sun and expended a lot of energy. But these days even office workers stop for a snack break, and schoolkids eat a mid-afternoon snack without fail, and often a mid-morning snack as well.

A merenda can be savory or sweet and rarely involves actual cooking, though wedges of unfussy, lightly sweetened home-baked desserts, such as a plain ciambellone ring cake or a jam tart, may be served for merenda. But most often a merenda is bread-based: a rosetta draped with a few slices of mortadella or prosciutto, a square of focaccia, a slice of toast spread with jam, or even just a piece of bread drizzled with olive oil and sprinkled with black pepper.

Almost every recipe in this chapter makes a good choice for merenda, and here are a few more ideas for humble yet satisfying snacks:

Butter a slice of bread and top with a couple of salted anchovy fillets (rinse them first!)
Rub a slice of toasted bread with the cut side of a tomato until the pulp penetrates
Blend ricotta with cocoa powder, spread on bread, and drizzle honey on top
Sprinkle a slice of bread with red wine and sugar
Apply a thin layer of gianduja (chocolate-hazelnut spread) to a slice of bread

BOMBOLONI AL GELATO
ICE CREAM SANDWICHES IN ITALIAN DOUGHNUTS

Makes 6 sandwiches

A fluffy bun split and filled with a scoop or two of gelato is a real treat—and a popular breakfast option in Italy, especially in Sicilia. We play off that tradition with an even more decadent option, a donut filled with ice cream. At Eataly we fry bomboloni in rice oil because it has such a neutral taste and high smoke point. You can find rice oil in Asian grocery stores, or use any other type of neutral oil, such as canola oil, that will not add any flavor to the bomboloni. In other words, skip the olive oil.

3 tablespoons plus 1 teaspoon whole milk

2 teaspoons instant yeast

2 cups unbleached bread flour

1 tablespoon plus 1 teaspoon sugar

1 large egg

1 tablespoon unsalted butter, softened

½ teaspoon salt

Neutral oil for frying

Confectioners' sugar for dusting

About 2 pints gelato of your choice

SCALD the milk and let it cool until warm. In a large bowl combine the yeast, flour, and sugar. Add the milk in a thin stream while stirring. Beat the egg and then add it to this mixture. Knead in the bowl until it forms a shaggy dough. Add the softened butter and knead in the bowl to incorporate, then transfer the dough to the work surface and knead until shiny and smooth, about 8 minutes. Sprinkle on the salt and knead until incorporated, 2 to 3 additional minutes. (Alternatively, knead the dough in a food processor fitted with the dough blade or a stand mixer fitted with the dough hook.)

TRANSFER the dough to a large bowl, cover tightly with plastic wrap, and allow to rise at room temperature until doubled in size, 1 to 2 hours.

DIVIDE the dough into six equal portions and shape each into a ball. Press down gently to flatten into disks, then place them on a board or plate with plenty of room between them, loosely cover (just rest a piece of plastic wrap on top of the balls), and let rise at room temperature until doubled and very puffy and extensible, about 1 hour.

LINE a sheet pan with paper towels, place a cooling rack on top, and set aside. Fill a high-sided pot with several inches of oil; clip a candy thermometer to the pot. Bring the oil in the pan to 350°F and fry the donuts.

WORK in batches to keep from crowding the pan and keep an eye on the oil temperature, adjusting the heat as needed. Fry until golden and puffed, turning once, 3 to 5 minutes per side. When the bomboloni are finished, with a skimmer remove to the prepared rack to drain. Wait for the oil temperature to return to 350°F and repeat with the remaining donuts.

WHEN the bomboloni are cool enough to handle (but still deliciously warm), dust with confectioners' sugar, split horizontally with a serrated knife, fill with gelato, and serve.

BISCOTTI AL GELATO

ICE CREAM SANDWICHES ON COOKIES

Makes 5 sandwiches

Spread ice cream between cookies for a portable treat, perfect for a cookout. We find these caramel cookies match beautifully with fig gelato, but experiment with various flavors to explore other combinations.

3 tablespoons plus 1 teaspoon heavy cream

1 cup plus 2 tablespoons packed brown sugar, plus more for work surface

2 tablespoons unsalted butter, softened

4½ cups unbleached all-purpose flour

1½ pints fig gelato or other gelato of your choosing

MAKE A DRY CARAMEL: Place the cream in a saucepan and heat until warm. Meanwhile, place a large pot over medium heat and 1 tablespoon at a time, add 1 cup of the brown sugar to the pan, stirring and waiting for the sugar to melt between additions. Adjust heat to guard against burning. When all the sugar has been incorporated and melted, carefully pour in the hot cream and stir to combine. Stir in the softened butter. When the butter is combined, add the flour and stir until combined. Remove from the heat and when the dough is cool enough to handle, knead briefly until smooth and uniform. Transfer the dough to a bowl, cover, and refrigerate for 2 hours.

AFTER 2 hours, knead the dough briefly on a clean work surface. Form it into 2 round logs each about 2¾ inches in diameter. Place the logs on a pan or platter, cover with plastic, and refrigerate for 30 minutes.

PREHEAT the oven to 350°F. Line two baking sheets or jelly roll pans with parchment paper and set aside. Sprinkle the remaining 2 tablespoons brown sugar on the work surface. Remove the dough logs from the refrigerator, brush them with water, and then roll them in the brown sugar so that they are coated on all sides.

CUT the logs into ¹⁄₁₀-inch-thick slices and arrange them on the prepared pans, leaving 1 inch between them. Bake until crisp, about 12 minutes. Cool the cookies on the pans on a rack.

TO make the sandwiches, allow the gelato to soften slightly at room temperature, about 10 minutes. Scoop some gelato and place on the flat side (bottom) of a cookie. Gently spread with an offset spatula. (If the gelato resists, try dipping the spatula blade in hot water then wiping it off.) Top with another cookie, flat side (bottom) against the gelato. Repeat with the remaining cookies and gelato. Wrap the sandwiches in wax paper and freeze until serving.

INDEX

Page references in *italics* refer to illustrations.

A

accavallato, or overlapped, bread shape, 131
Altamura, pane di, 131
appetizers:
   Cheese-Stuffed Focaccia from Recco (focaccia di Recco), 101–4, *102–5*
   Chickpea Flour Flatbread (farinata), 113
   crostini and bruschette, 157
   Tramezzini, 150, *151*
   Truffle Pizza (pizza al tartufo), 52, *53*–54
Apulia, *see* Puglia
Arezzo, pan co' grifi of, 142
Artichoke Pizza (pizza ai carciofini), 56–57
arugula, 84
   Panuozzo, 163
   Piadina with Fresh Cheese and (piadina con formaggio fresco e rucola), 158–59
   Star-Shaped Pizza (pizza stella), *40*, 41–42
   in topping and filling combinations, 86, 143, 146, 150
Asiago, 146

B

bacon, pizza alla pala with egg and, 86
baking stones, 107
Bari:
   pizza traditional to, 12
   -Style Focaccia with Tomatoes, Olives, and Oregano (focaccia barese), *108*, 109–10, *110*
beef:
   cured meats, 140, *141*
   Prime Rib Sandwich (panino di manza), *152*, 153
bench scrapers, 107
Bergamo, bread unique to (stellina), 131
berries, in Sweet Focaccia (focaccia dolce), 118–20, *119*
biga (pre-ferment or starter dough), 8
Biscotti al Gelato (ice cream sandwiches on cookies), 168–69
black pepper, in Cacio e Pepe Pizza, 46–48, *47*
Bolzano, pane di, 131
Bomboloni al Gelato (ice cream sandwiches in Italian doughnuts), 165–66, *167*
bread flour, 18
breads, 131
   Country-Style (pane rustico), 125–26, *127*
   Sandwich (pane in cassetta), 147–48, *149*
   see also flatbreads; focaccia; pizza; rolls
bresaola, 140, *141*
bruschette, 157
Brussels sprouts and pancetta pizza alla pala, 86
buratto flour, 18
burrata, 146
   pizza alla pala with tomatoes and, 86

C

caciocavallo, 146
Cacio e Pepe Pizza, 46–48, *47*
Caffè Mulassano, Torino, 147
Calabria:
   breads unique to (pitta china and other forms of pitta), 95, 131
   morzello of, 142
Calzone, 36, 37–38, *39*
cannellini, crostini con, 157
cappello di prete, or priest's hat, bread shape, 131
carbonara, as pizza topping, 49
carrots, pizza alla pala with ricotta and, 86
Caseificio Olanda, Andria, Puglia, 32
Catanzaro, morzello of, 142
cheese(s):
   Cacio e Pepe Pizza, 46–48, *47*
   -forward pizzas, what to drink with, 74
   Fresh, Piadina with Arugula and (piadina con formaggio fresco e rucola), 158–59
   goat, in Thin Double-Crust Pizza from Gaeta (tiella di formaggio), 68
   pizza ai cinque formaggi, 49
   for sandwiches, 146
   -Stuffed Focaccia from Recco, 101–4, *102–5*
chicken liver pâté, in crostini toscani, 157
chickpea flour, 18
   Flatbread (farinata), 113
   fritters, in pane e panelle, 142
chocolate, in Sweet Focaccia (focaccia dolce), 118–20, *119*
ciabatta, 131
Cookies, Ice Cream Sandwiches on (biscotti al gelato), 168–69
coppa, or capocolla, 140
Country-Style Bread (pane rustico), 125–26, *127*
crescentine, also known as tigelle, 160
   Modena Stovetop Flatbreads (crescentine modenesi), 161
crescia sfogliata, 160
crescioni, also known as cassoni, 160
crostini, 157
cucina povera, 142
culatello di zibello, 140
cured meats, 140, *141*
cutters, 107

D

desserts:
   Grape Schiacciata (schiacciata all'uva), 114–17, *115–17*

Ice Cream Sandwiches in Italian Doughnuts (bomboloni al gelato), 165–66, *167*
Ice Cream Sandwiches on Cookies (biscotti al gelato), 168–69
Sweet Focaccia (focaccia dolce), 118–20, *119*
Doughnuts, Italian, Ice Cream Sandwiches in (bomboloni al gelato), 165–66, *167*
Dumplings, Fried (gnocco fritto), 162

E

egg, pizza alla pala with bacon and, 86
eggplant, in Thin Double-Crust Pizza from Gaeta (tiella di melanzane), 68
escarole, in Thin Double-Crust Pizza from Gaeta (tiella di scarola), 68

F

farina 0 and farina 00, 18
Farinata (chickpea flour flatbread), 113
fermentation (first rise), 8, 14–15
Filoncini (long rolls), 128–30, *129*
finocchiona, 140, *141*
flatbreads:
　Chickpea Flour (farinata), 113
　Piadina with Fresh Cheese and Arugula (piadina con formaggio fresco e rucola), 158–59
　stovetop, 160
　Stovetop, Modena (crescentine modenesi), 161
Florence (Firenze):
　lampredotto of, 142
　pizza traditional to, 12
flours, 18
focaccia, 90–95, 101–10, 114–21
　Bari-Style, with Tomatoes, Olives, and Oregano (focaccia barese), 108, 109–10, *110*
　Cheese-Stuffed, from Recco (focaccia di Recco), 101–4, *102–5*
　Grape Schiacciata (schiacciata all'uva), 114–17, *115–17*
　how to form, 92, *92*
　pan breads similar to, 95
　regional traditions, 12
　with Rosemary and Salt (focaccia genovese), 90–91
　sliced and filled (focaccia farcita), 143, *143*
　Sweet (focaccia dolce), 118–21, *119*, *120*
　Thin, from Voltri (focaccia di Voltri), 93–94
　with various toppings, 96–97
fontina, 146
food processor, kneading dough in, 88
Forlì, pizza traditional to, 12
four seasons pizza (quattro stagioni), 28, *29*
fried:
　Dumplings (gnocco fritto), 162
　Panzerotti, 111–12
　Pizza (pizza fritta), 43–44

G

Gaeta, Thin Double-Crust Pizza from (tiella di Gaeta), 66–68
garlic, in bruschette all'aglio, 157
gelato:
　Biscotti al (ice cream sandwiches on cookies), 168–69
　Bomboloni al (ice cream sandwiches in Italian doughnuts), 165–66, *167*
Genoa (Genova):
　Focaccia with Rosemary and Salt (focaccio genovese), 90–91
　pizza traditional to, 12
Gnocco Fritto (fried dumplings), 162
goat cheese, in Thin Double-Crust Pizza from Gaeta (tiella di formaggio), 68
Grape Schiacciata (schiacciata all'uva), 114–17, *115–17*

H

hands, working and shaping dough with, 107

I

ice cream sandwiches:
　on Cookies (biscotti al gelato), 168–69
　in Italian Doughnuts (bomboloni al gelato), 165–66, *167*
impasto per la pizza:
　di Eataly, 10–11
　al Padellino, 61–62
　alla Pala, 80
innards, in regional sandwich traditions, 142

K

kneading dough, 88–89

L

lampredotto, 142
lardo, 140, *141*
lemon ricotta pizza alla pala, 86
lievito madre (mother yeast), 15, 16
Liguria:
　Cheese-Stuffed Focaccia from Recco (focaccia di Recco), 101–4, *102–5*
　Chickpea Flour Flatbread (farinata), 113
　Lombardy, bread unique to (ciabatta), 131
　Long Rolls (filoncini), 128–30, *129*

M

mafalda, 131
Marche:
　crescia sfogliata from, 160
　panino con le spuntature from, 142
　prosciutto from, 140
Margherita, Queen of Savoy, 23, *25*
Margherita pizza:
　as base for other toppings, 28, *29*
　al padellino, 64
　TSG (pizza Margherita verace STG), 25–26, *27*
Marinara Pizza, 33–34
　al padellino, 64

INDEX

meat-based pizzas, what to drink with, 74
merenda, 164
Messina, focaccia traditional to (focaccia messinese), 95
michetta, 131
Milan (Milano):
   bread uniqie to (michetta), 131
   pizza traditional to, 12
Modena:
   prosciutto from, 140
   Stovetop Flatbreads (crescentine modenesi), 161
montanara, 43
mortadella, 140, *141*
morzello, or morzeddu, 142
mozzarella, 146
   di bufala, 30
   fior di latte, 32
   Panuozzo, 163
   Panzerotti, 111–12
   and Tomato Sandwich (panino caprese), *144*, 145
   white pizza (pizza bianca), 30
mushroom(s):
   pizza (pizza con funghi), 29
   pizzas, what to drink with, 74
   in topping combinations, 12, 29

N

Naples (Napoli):
   Calzone, *36*, 37–38, *39*
   Fried Pizza (pizza fritta), 43–44
   Neapolitan pizza (pizza napoletana), 23–34, *45*
      Dough, 24
      Margherita, as base for toppings, 28, *29*
      Margherita, TSG (pizza Margherita verace STG), 25–26, *27*
      Marinara, 33–34
      tradition and heritage of, 23
      wallet pizza (pizza a portafoglio), 32

O

occhi di Santa Lucia, or Saint Lucy's eyes, bread shape, 131
octopus, in Thin Double-Crust Pizza from Gaeta (tiella di Gaeta), 66–67
olive oil, 98–100
   how to taste, 100
   information on bottle, 99
Olives, Bari-Style Focaccia with Tomatoes, Oregano and (focaccia barese), *108*, 109–10, *110*
onion:
   Pizza with Radicchio and (pizza radicchio e cipolla), 20, 21–22
   and Tuna Pizza (pizza tonno e cipolla), 50–51
organ meats, in regional sandwich traditions, 142

P

Palermo:
   pane con la milza of, 142
   pane e panelle of, 142
pancetta and Brussels sprouts pizza alla pala, 86
pan co' grifi, 142
pane con la milza, 142
pane di Altamura, 131
pane di Bolzano, 131
pane e panelle, 142
Pane in Cassetta (sandwich bread), 147–48, *149*
Pane Rustico (country-style bread), 125–26, *127*
pane sciocco, 131
panini, 123–69
   see also ice cream sandwices; rolls; sandwiches
panini grigliati, 155
Panini Soffici, 138–39, *139*
Panino Caprese (mozzarella and tomato sandwich), *144*, 145
panino con le spuntature, 142
Panino di Manza (prime rib sandwich), *152*, 153
Panino di Porchetta (porchetto sandwich), 154–55
pan pizza, *see* pizza al padellino
pans, 107
Panuozzo, 163
Panzerotti, 111–12
Parmigiano Reggiano, 146
pasta sauces transformed into pizza toppings:
   Cacio e Pepe Pizza, 46–48, *47*
   pizza ai cinque formaggi, 49
   pizza alla gricia, 49
   pizza all'Amatriciana, 49
   pizza carbonara, 49
Pasta Sfoglia per Pizzette, 70–71
peas, in crostini con piselli, 157
pecorino, 146
peels, 107
Pepper, Sausage, and Onion Pizza alla Pala, 81–83, *82–83*
piadina:
   with Fresh Cheese and Arugula (piadina con formaggio fresco e rucola), 158–59
   regional differeces in, 159
piave, 146
pitta, 131
pitta china, 95
pizza:
   all'Amatriciana, 49
   Artichoke (pizza ai carciofini), 56–57
   by the slice (al taglio), 78; *see also* pizza alla pala
   Cacio e Pepe, 46–48, *47*
   capricciosa, 29
   carbonara, 49
   ai cinque formaggi, 49
   crisp-crust round, of Rome (pizza romana tonda), *45*, 45
   four seasons (quattro stagioni), 28, *29*
   Fried (pizza fritta), 43–44
   alla gricia, 49
   Margherita, as base for other toppings, 28, *29*
   Margherita, TSG (pizza Margherita verace STG), 25–26, *27*
   Marinara, 33–34
   mushroom (pizza con funghi), 29
   Neapolitan (pizza napoletana), tradition and heritage of, 23

pizza continued:
  with Radicchio and Onion (pizza radicchio e cipolla), 20, 21–22
  red or white (rossa o bianca), 30
  regional traditions, 12
  romana, 33
  Salami, Spicy (pizza massese), 58, 59–60
  Star-Shaped (pizza stella), 40, 41–42
  Truffle (pizza al tartufo), 52, 53–54
  Tuna and Onion (pizza tonno e cipolla), 50–51
  wallet (pizza a portafoglio), 32
  what to drink with, 74
Pizza, Thin Double-Crust, from Gaeta (tiella di Gaeta), 66–68
  escarole (tiella di scarola), 68
  goat cheese (tiella di formaggio), 68
  with octopus cooked in its own juices (tiella di polpo cotto nella sua acqua), 67
  squid (tiella di calamari), 67
pizza alla pala, 78–87
  Bacon and Egg, 86
  Brussels Sprouts and Pancetta, 87
  with Burrata and Tomatoes, 86
  with Carrots and Ricotta, 87
  Dough for, 80
  Lemon Ricotta, 87
  Salmon, 86
  Sausage, Pepper, and Onion, 81–83, 82–83
  Squash, 87
  Three-Color, 86
  three types of toppings for, 84
  White, 86
pizza al padellino (individual pan pizza with a thick crust, also known as pizza al tegamino), 61–64
  favorite topping combinations for, 64, 65

  Pan Pizza Dough for, 61–62, 63
pizza dough:
  Eataly (recipe), 10–11
  Neapolitan, 24
  Pan (pizza al padellino, or pizza al tegamino), 61–62
  stretching into circle, 17
  yeast, fermentation, and rising of, 14–16
Pizza Sandwich (panuozzo), 163
pizzaiolo, or pizza maker, 72
pizzette, 69–71
  Puff Pastry for (pasta sfoglia per pizzette), 70–71
  toppings for, 69
Porchetta Sandwich (panino di porchetta), 154–55
pork:
  cured meats, 140, *141*
  Porchetta Sandwich (panino di porchetta), 154–55
  Spicy Salami Pizza (pizza massese), 58, 59–60
Prime Rib Sandwich (panino di manza), 152, 153
prosciutto, DOP, types of, 140
prosciutto cotta, 140
prosciutto crudo, *141*
prosciutto di Parma, in Panuozzo, 163
provolone, 146
puff pastry:
  for Pizzette (pasta sfoglia per pizzette), 70–71
  quick (pasta sfoglia veloce), 71
Puglia (Apulia):
  Bari-Style Focaccia with Tomatoes, Olives, and Oregano (focaccia barese), 108, 109–10, *110*
  bread unique to (pane di Altamura), 131
Panzerotti, 111–12

R

Radicchio, Pizza with Onion and (pizza radicchio e cipolla), 20, 21–22

Recco, Cheese-Stuffed Focaccia from (focaccia di Recco), 101–4, *102–5*
ricotta, 146
  bruschette siciliane, 157
  lemon pizza alla pala, 86
  pizza alla pala with carrots and, 86
  pizza al padellino with zucchini and, 64, *65*
robiola, 146
rolls, *see* sandwich rolls
Romagna:
  crescioni of, 160
  piadine flatbreads of, 158–59
Rome (Roma):
  Cacio e Pepe Pizza, 46–48, *47*
  crisp-crust round pizza of (pizza romana tonda), 45, *45*
  pizza traditional to, 12
Rosemary, Focaccia with Salt and (focaccia genovese), 90–91
Rosetta Rolls, 131, *132*, 133–34, *135–36*
rye flour:
  in lievito madre (mother yeast), 16
  pane di Bolzano, 131

S

salame Felino, 140
salame Milano, 140
Salami Pizza, Spicy (pizza massese), 58, 59–60
salmon pizza alla pala, 86
salt, 131
salumi (cured meats), 140, *141*
Sandwich Bread (pane in cassetta), 147–48, *149*
sandwiches (panini), 123–69
  cheeses for, 146
  cured meats for, 140, *141*
  morzello, 146
  Mozzarella and Tomato (panino caprese), 144, 145
  open-faced (crostini and bruschette), 157
  origins of, 124
  pane con la milza, 146
  pane e panelle, 146

panino con le spuntature, 142
Porchetta (panino di porchetta), 154–55
Prime Rib (panino di manza), 152, 153
regional traditions, 142
Tramezzini, 150, 151
warm pressed (panini grigliati), 155
see also ice cream sandwiches
sandwich rolls:
  Long (filoncini), 128–30, 129
  Rosetta (rosette), 131, 132, 133–34, 135–36
  Soft (panini soffici), 138–39, 139
San Remo, sardenaira of, 95
sardenaira, also known as piscialandrea, 95
Sausage, Pepper, and Onion Pizza alla Pala, 81–83, 82–83
Schiacciata, Grape (schiacciata all'uva), 114–17, 115–17
semolina flour (semola rimacinata), 18
  Bari-Style Focaccia with Tomatoes, Olives, and Oregano (focaccia barese), 108, 109–10, 110
  pane di Altamura, 131
  Panzerotti, 111–12
  Sicilian (mafalda), 131
sfincione, 95
Sicily (Sicilia), 165
  bruschette siciliane, 157
  focaccia Messinese, 95
  mafalda, 131
  sfincione, 95
snacks, 164
  Chickpea Flour Flatbread (farinata), 113
  crostini and bruschette, 157
soppressata, also known as testa in cassetta, 140
  pizza al padellino with, 64
speck, 140, 141
Spicy Salami Pizza (pizza massese), 58, 59–60
squash:
  crostini con zucca, 157
  pizza alla pala, 86

squid, in Thin Double-Crust Pizza from Gaeta (tiella di calamari), 68
stand mixer, kneading dough in, 88
Star-Shaped Pizza (pizza stella), 40, 41–42
stellina, 131
stesura, 17
stovetop flatbreads, 160–61
  Modena (crescentine modenesi), 161
stracchino, 146
Sweet Focaccia (focaccia dolce), 118–20, 119

T
tartufo (truffles), 55, 55
  pizza al (Truffle Pizza), 52, 53–54
terroir, water and, 137
Tiella di Gaeta, 66–68
tomato(es):
  Bari-Style Focaccia with Olives, Oregano and (focaccia barese), 108, 109–10, 110
  -based pizzas, what to drink with, 74
  bruschette al pomodoro, 157
  and Mozzarella Sandwich (panino caprese), 144, 145
  Pizza Marinara, 33–34
  red pizza (pizza rossa), 30
Torino:
  pizza al padellino of, 61–64, 63
  pizza traditional to, 12
torta al testo, 160
Traditional Specialty Guaranteed (TSG) certification, 23, 26
Tramezzini, 150, 151
  invention of, 147
  Sandwich Bread for (pane in cassetta), 147–48, 149
Trieste, pizza traditional to, 12
truffle(s) (tartufo), 55, 55
  Pizza (pizza al tartufo), 52, 53–54

tuna:
  crostini con tonno, 157
  and Onion Pizza (pizza tonno e cipolla), 50–51
turnovers:
  Calzone, 36, 37–38, 39
  Fried Pizza (pizza fritta), 43–44
  Panzerotti, 111–12
Tuscany (Toscana):
  bread unique to (pane sciocco), 131
  crostini with chicken liver pâté, 157
  prosciutto from, 140

U
Umbria, torta al testo of, 160

V
Voltri, Thin Focaccia from, 93–94

W
water, 8, 137
white beans, in crostini con cannellini, 157
white pizza (pizza bianca), 30
  Artichoke (pizza ai carciofini), 56–57
  Cacio e Pepe, 46–48, 47
  carbonara, 49
  ai cinque formaggi, 49
  alla gricia, 49
  alla pala, 86
  Truffle (pizza al tartufo), 52, 53–54
  what to drink with, 74
whole wheat flour, 18
wood oven, 9

Y
yeast, 14–16
  fermentation (first rise) and, 8, 14–15
  forms of, 14, 15
  mother (lievito madre), 15, 16
  storing, 15
  water temperature and, 137

Z
zucchini, pizza al padellino with ricotta and, 64, 65

First published in the United States of America in 2021 by
Rizzoli International Publications, Inc.
300 Park Avenue South
New York, NY 10010
rizzoliusa.com

© 2021 by Eataly, Inc.

Text: Natalie Danford
Photography: Francesco Sapienza, FrancescoSapienza.com
Prop Styling: Maeve Sheridan

Publisher: Charles Miers
Editors: Jono Jarrett, Rachel Goodman, James Taylor
Design: Vertigo Design NYC
Production Manager: Kaija Markoe
Managing Editor: Lynn Scrabis

All rights reserved. No part of this publication may be reproduced, stored in a retrieval system, or transmitted in any form or by any means, electronic, mechanical, photocopying, recording, or otherwise, without prior consent of the publishers.

Printed in China
2021 2022 2023 2024 / 10 9 8 7 6 5 4 3 2 1

ISBN: 978-0-8478-6876-6
Library of Congress Control Number: 2021934019

Visit us online:
Facebook.com/RizzoliNewYork
Twitter: @Rizzoli_Books
Instagram.com/RizzoliBooks
Pinterest.com/RizzoliBooks
Youtube.com/user/RizzoliNY